Praise for SELF HELP JESUS

"Dan Matthews' *Self Help Jesus* illuminates the core teachings of Jesus the Christ on personal transformation and the innate capacities of the human heart. Enjoy this nourishing and healing book."

~ Michael Bernard Beckwith, author of *Spiritual Liberation*

"*Self Help Jesus* is an insightful and uplifting book that connects spirituality and personal growth. Dan Matthews shares with us his unique perspective on the benefits of combining religion and personal development. He explains how you can reach higher levels of prosperity by combining universal truths, God's Love, and personal development. I recommend it to anyone wishing to bring more abundance into their lives."

~ Peggy McColl, *New York Times* Best Selling Author

"This is a fun and intriguing read! Mixing stories of life and the teachings of Jesus with physical and spiritual laws, Dan Matthews has woven a book full of practical inspiration for every reader. I look forward to reading the remaining books in his "The Ancient Masters of Personal Development" series!"

~ Blaine Bartlett, Best Selling Author of *Compassionate Capitalism: A Journey to the Soul of Business*

"Dan Matthews presents the nature of God, classical and quantum laws of physics, biology and spiritual laws, all in one delicious mix that teaches, inspires and connects the Bible with modern life in a new and very personal way."

~ Judy O'Beirn, Creator of the International Bestselling series *Unwavering Strength*.

"Over 2,000 years ago a very wise man walked this earth. Dan is introducing you to the words of this man, in a different light. A light you may have never experienced before. Will you agree with what he has written in these pages? Open your mind, open your heart, read the book and then decide. You'll be glad you did!"

~ Julie Smithwick, Best Selling Author and Awareness Expert

"Self Help Jesus" is a unique manuscript that, as a modern day personal development coach, I found inspirational and thought provoking. God is love. We are love, and Jesus taught this from a very high level of consciousness. We as humans desire spiritual growth – but not all of us have It figured out yet. I really enjoyed reading this and gleaning every bit of knowledge it had to offer. I have always had a deep reverence for the teachings of the Bible about Jesus – it's well worth the read and will truly bless you in years to come with treasures of wisdom in abundance"

> ~ Jennie Lynn, #1 Bestselling Author of *Magnetic Love*

"God is love. This we know. Faith without works is dead. This we also know, but it can be tricky to love and to have faith in today's modern world. What does having faith really mean? How do I love when I've been so hurt? This is where *Self Help Jesus* comes in. A practical look at Jesus' teachings and how to apply them in your life today. Bravo Dan!"

> ~ Colleen Aynn, International Bestselling author of the children's book series *Feeling Friends*. Professional Speaker Coach and creator of the EPIC System. www.colleenaynn.com

"This book is a beautiful mix of science and theology which Dan Matthews brings together so eloquently. He shows clearly how Jesus might in the present day be called a life coach, and how He worked to get his message across to people. Religions have far more in common than differences, and I applaud Dan for his decision to show the similarities. I look forward to the rest of the series.

Awareness of the core values in all religions can only lead us towards a more peaceful world."

> ~ Lisa Bowen, Author of *Finding the Gorgeous in You: A Toolbox for Life*

CREATING ABUNDANCE BY APPLYING SPIRITUAL LAWS

SELF HELP
JESUS

DAN R. MATTHEWS

Published by
Hasmark Publishing, judy@hasmarkservices.com

Copyright © 2018 Dan R. Matthews
First Edition, 2018

No part of this book may be reproduced or transmitted in any form or by any means, electronic or mechanical, including photocopying, recording, or by any information storage and retrieval system, without written permission from the author, except for the inclusion of brief quotations in a review.

Disclaimer

This book is designed to provide information and motivation to our readers. It is sold with the understanding that the publisher is not engaged to render any type of psychological, legal, or any other kind of professional advice. The content of each article is the sole expression and opinion of its author and not necessarily that of the publisher. No warranties or guarantees are expressed or implied by the publisher's choice to include any of the content in this volume. Neither the publisher nor the individual author(s) shall be liable for any physical, psychological, emotional, financial, or commercial damages, including, but not limited to, special, incidental, consequential, or other damages. Our views and rights are the same: you are responsible for your own choices, actions, and results.

Permission should be addressed in an email to Dan R. Matthews: prosperity@danrmatthews.com

Editor, Nita Robinson
Nita Helping Hand?
nita@nitahelpinghand.com

Cover Design, Patti Knowles

Book Design, Anne Karklins
annekarklins@gmail.com

ISBN 978-1-988071-86-2
ISBN 1988071860

With Gratitude

To Sharen, for her support, commitment and companionship along our path

ACKNOWLEDGEMENTS

Several people have been instrumental in helping this book come into being. First, thanks to Sharen for her support, encouragement and helpful input. Thank you to Bob Proctor and Peggy McColl for inspiration at the inception and instruction along the way. Lisa Bowen and Victoria Ramirez read early drafts of the manuscript and offered valuable feedback. Thanks to everyone who graciously endorsed the book. Colin Miller did a superb job building the web site. Anthony and Gillis Bratsch did a phenomenal job creating compelling promotional videos. The team at Hasmark was instrumental in bringing the book into its finished form, and in presenting it to readers world-wide.

Table of Contents

Introduction	1
Chapters	
Part One: The Nature of God	7
Endless	9
Everywhere	13
All Powerful	18
All Knowing	19
Seeing Within: The Heart of the Matter	26
The Kingdom of Heaven is Within You	30
Part Two: The Physical Laws of Nature	33
Fundamentally Undefinable	35
Action and Reaction: The Third Law of Motion	38
Conservation of Energy	40
Entropy: Expansion and Decay	44
Waves: Vibration and Frequency	46
Resonance and Harmony	50
Communication by Vibration	53
Attraction and Repulsion	60
The Quantum World and Thought	63
Part Three: Spiritual Laws of the Universe	67
Divine Oneness: I AM, Energy IS	69
Correspondence: As Above, So Below	73
Perpetual Transmutation of Energy	76
Vibration	78
Attraction	81
Cause and Effect	92

Polarity and Relativity	103
Rhythm	109
Gender and Gestation	113
Part Four: Achieving Abundance: Applying the Laws	**119**
Expansion and Growth	121
The Expanding Dream	123
Why Am I Here?	126
Purpose	126
Vision and the Path	129
Setting Goals	132
Courage, Fear and Love	135
Getting Through the Rough Spots	141
Persistence	141
Focus	143
Create the Image Then Make it Real	146
Repetition	150
The Power of Gratitude, Love and Giving Back	153
Gratitude	153
Love	154
Giving Back	156
Opportunity	158
The Power of Faith, Belief and Expectation	160
Faith and Belief	160
Expectation	167
A Vision of Success	170
Forgiveness	172
About the Author	**175**

Introduction

If your goal is to find love, first seek love. Then allow love to find you.

And we have known and believed the love that God hath to us. God is love; and he that dwelleth in love dwelleth in God, and God in him. – I John 4:16

…God is Love…

This has been said in many different ways, all around the earth. Love is the answer. It doesn't matter which religion or philosophy, or exactly what words are used. God is Love is the fundamental truth of all religions. But just a step away from this fundamental truth, religions of the world start to disagree. The focus changes from Love to interpretations of meaning. What should be tiny nuances are made into complicated rules that actually obscure the truth that God is Love. Energy that should flow freely from heaven to humans is clogged with the debris of personality, politics and prejudice. The light that is intended to radiate into our hearts with infinite healing power becomes dim, and we humans are left in the twilight with just a memory of the truth. Dogma overrides divine blessing. Understanding dwindles. Disagreements, even within the same religion, lead to separation. Love is set aside and replaced by its polar opposite, fear. The history of civilization shows the results. "God is Love" has become completely reversed, almost forgotten.

But imagine this: What if we could retrace our steps, back to the day when the idea "God is Love" was all we needed? How would the world be different? What if we could see how religions are similar, and how they each bring similar values to humanity? Commonality is at the core of every religion, even today. Every religion tells the story of becoming a better person, giving, accepting and seeking the kingdom of heaven.

Jesus said it very simply. When He was asked which was the greatest law, He answered:

> *Thou shalt love the Lord thy God with all thy heart, and with all thy soul, and with all thy mind. This is the first and great commandment. And the second is like unto it, Thou shalt love thy neighbour as thyself. On these two commandments hang all the law and the prophets.* – Matthew 22:37-40

It's all about love. It always has been. If we as a human community focused on love and understanding, and on what we share with others in our community, we could change the course of history. This change would require a journey over some difficult paths, but it is a journey and a goal, I believe, worth pursuing.

Besides "God is Love," what else do the great religions agree upon? There are many things; so many that the emphasis could just as well be on the similarities instead of the differences. We could celebrate qualities that we share around the world, that bring us together as humans; qualities like acceptance, kindness, finding purpose in life, and personal growth. At the deepest level of the heart we are all the same. It doesn't matter if we live in Dallas or Mumbai, Beijing or Nairobi.

Each of us has goals, dreams, and fears. Life's challenges and struggles, successes and failures are common themes around the world. We all desire to be loved, to have deep and meaningful relationships, to prosper, grow and make the world a better place for ourselves and our children. Our common values can bring us together, open our awareness, and move the earth to a higher level of prosperity, unity and gratitude.

But how does this opening of awareness and growth come about?

The Ancient Masters, upon whose teachings the great religions are built, knew the fundamental truth that God, by whatever name we choose, is Love. They also knew that every person has the ability to become better than what they are. We can all become more spiritual, more understanding and more prosperous.

The intention of this first book is to focus on Jesus as a teacher. Jesus completely understood that the nature of God is love and Infinite Responsive Intelligence. He knew that God exists in all places, at all times, and contains all knowledge. He also knew that communication with God and the achievement of worthy goals could be achieved by following unchanging spiritual laws. In order to teach these truths, Jesus needed to explain abstract concepts like infinity, omnipresence and immutable spiritual laws to people who knew precious little about the wheel, primitive tools or agriculture, and nothing about the world as we know it today. So Jesus spoke simply, to their hearts. In plain language, He often used parables to present a deep concept by telling a simple story. He explained the nature of God in terms which the people of His day could understand. Using the familiar image of a parent and child, Jesus illustrated the compassion and love of God. People who truly listened learned how to get into communication with God, and learned how God desires to make every person more loving, more grateful and more prosperous. Jesus encouraged people to look within themselves to find strength and love. He taught about applying spiritual laws to receive the abundance that God has to give. Using simple lessons, Jesus showed how any of us can come into harmony with God, by looking within.

... behold, the kingdom of God is within you. – Luke 17:21

If Jesus walked the earth today, he might be called a personal development coach. His teachings still inspire us to look within ourselves, to seek growth and improvement, to be successful, and to believe that we can achieve goals in life. He taught that through faith and gratitude, we can expand and grow to a higher level of existence by performing acts of kindness, by giving love to others. He taught that each of us is meant to grow and to live a more abundant life. He encouraged each of us to ask for what seems to be impossible.

We know that God is not an elderly man with long hair, muscles and a beard, lounging in the clouds as Michelangelo depicted five hundred years ago. The entity we call God is spirit, Infinite Intelligence, which is entirely present in all time and all space, unchanged since the beginning of the universe. God is called many names: universal intelligence, cosmic awareness, the I Am, the Word, Allah, the Great Spirit, Jaweh, or a number of other names. We are told that God is Spirit.

> *God is Spirit: and they that worship him must worship him in spirit and in truth.* – John 4:24

> *I speak to the world those things which I have heard of him (God, Infinite Intelligence).* – John 8:26

This book is divided into four general parts. The first part focuses on the qualities of God, Infinite Intelligence, as we understand them. Some of the physical Laws of Nature that govern our tangible world are briefly described in the second part. The third portion addresses the intangible but very real Spiritual Laws, counterparts of the Physical Laws. The fourth section looks at achieving abundance and attaining goals by applying the Spiritual Laws.

We will look at God and some of the teachings of Jesus from a new perspective, and see how Jesus' teachings can be used today to inspire our own personal development. Jesus taught that the kingdom of God is within each of us. Abundance, understanding and worthy goals are ours for the asking.

The Bible has been translated many times, and there are questions about the accuracy of some of the translations when compared to early documents. These are issues with which this book is not concerned. The translation chosen for the verses referenced is the King James Version, first printed in 1611, the time of Shakespeare, when the New World was really new.

Come with me on a journey. In the words of Jesus,

> *If thou canst believe, all things are possible.* – Mark 9:23

And so begins the journey,
That one calls mystical,
Another, foolish and deluded.
But who shall know the truth?
At first, it's just a few steps
Much like any other

Taken on a quiet cloudy morning,
Until the Threshold is reached,
The Door opened,
And beyond, a new world
Where there are no names
For the millions of new things
Never seen, never touched, never breathed,
And no path leading from the Doorway.
Not a footprint on the ground.
So what do we call this Moment,
This Journey?

> ...*prove me now herewith, saith the LORD of hosts, if I will not open you the windows of heaven, and pour you out a blessing, that there shall not be room enough to receive it.*
> – Malachi 3:10

PART ONE:
THE NATURE OF GOD

Endless

Do not fear the unknown heights, but embrace the air, and fly.

Heaven and earth shall pass away, but my words shall not pass away. – Matthew 24:35, Mark 13:31, Luke 21:33

Here is an old riddle, slightly amended:
The beginning of eternity, the end of time and space
The beginning of every end, and the end of every race.
In life and death, in love and dreams, just look – you'll find me there
In heaven, hell and gratitude, in hope and in despair.
What am I?

One of the characteristics of God is that of being infinite. Infinite Intelligence. Infinity is a big subject, and it makes some people uncomfortable. It is, after all, larger than anything we can imagine. We feel like we live in a finite world, and in many ways that is true. Our days are divided up into day and night. A life span is a long time for humans, but we know that human history extends back millions of years. Our earth seems huge. But it is nowhere close to being infinite, either in time or in space. Getting our minds around the concept of endless space and time is a very large task.

…throughout all ages, world without end. Amen. – Ephesians 3:21

One day in a physics class which I was teaching, we started a discussion about the number of hydrogen atoms in one gram of hydrogen. That number is called one Mole, and is very big. Written out, it is the number 6, followed by twenty-three zeroes! As I introduced this concept, I noticed one student's face flush, eyes welling with tears. I asked, "Are you OK?"

The student's answer was surprising. "Is this something like infinity, that no matter how hard you try, you can't understand it?"

I went a little further. "Is this a little scary for you?"

"Yes, a little bit," the student replied.

When we come face to face with something that is unimaginably large and endless, it makes our life on earth seem insignificant and very temporary. The idea of infinity can be frightening, but that's only one way of looking at the universe. We will spend a little time looking at it this way, then make a shift in our perspective.

Let's go back to that number of hydrogen atoms. How large a number is it? How close is it to infinity? To get a clearer picture, look at this number in everyday terms. Think of a hydrogen atom as a grain of sand.

Imagine you use this sand to make a beach. That beach would be about 500 feet deep, half a mile wide, and would extend over 1500 miles. That's a beach almost as long as the east coast of the United States, and that's about the number of hydrogen atoms in one gram! Atoms are far too small to be seen, but the number of them in a building, or the entire earth, or in the galaxy, is really overwhelming. And the whole galaxy is only a tiny speck in the universe. It's no wonder my student felt a little uneasy!

Even if the number of atoms in the entire universe could be estimated, that number would not be infinite. God, Infinite Intelligence, is many times larger. Infinitely larger.

> *But will God indeed dwell on the earth? Behold, the heaven and heaven of heavens cannot contain thee...* – I Kings 8:27

We can also look at the idea of infinity in terms of distance. Our normal experience of distance and time mean nothing when compared with infinity. Consider the largest distances that astronomers have studied. Is distance in the universe infinite?

> *And the earth was without form, and void; and darkness was upon the face of the deep. And the Spirit of God moved upon the face of the waters. And God said, Let there be light: and there was light. And God saw the light, that it was good: and God divided the light from the darkness. Genesis 1:2-4*

Astronomers have several ways of measuring distances between the stars and galaxies. One way uses visible light. Most families have a pair of binoculars in the house, and some have small telescopes, sometimes called "spotting scopes," used by nature lovers and hunters. Large astronomical observatories may have radio telescopes, which do not use visible light. These huge telescopes detect radio frequencies of light, much like a gigantic array of car radios. Still other telescopes detect ultraviolet radiation or x-rays. All of these telescopes have one thing in common. They detect electromagnetic radiation coming into the earth from the heavens.

As astronomers use their telescopes to search the heavens, they "see" objects farther and farther away. The only limit to how far away objects can be seen appears to be the limit that comes from the speed that light travels. There appears to be an "optical edge" to the visible universe, and that edge is far, far away, as they say in Hollywood. How far away is this visible edge of the universe? Think about this for a moment.

Light travels very fast. 186,000 miles (300,000 km) per second. Humans have never come close to that speed. Astronauts have travelled about 20,000 miles per hour, but the speed of light is over 30,000 times faster than that! You probably learned in grade school that it takes sunlight about eight minutes to reach the earth. That distance is less than one hundred million miles. Distances in astronomy are measured in units called Light Years, which is the distance that light travels in one year. That distance is almost six trillion miles. For an astronaut at today's speeds to travel one light year would take over 30,000 years, one way.

The galaxy we live in, the Milky Way, is about 150,000 light years across. One of our nearby neighboring galaxies, Andromeda, is about 2.5 million light years away from the Milky Way. So how far is it to the visible edge of the universe? The estimated distance is about fourteen billion light years. So, is this close to an infinite distance? Not exactly.

There are two interesting side stories here. One of them is that the visible edge of the universe appears to be getting farther away all the time. The universe is expanding unimaginably fast. The second story is that many astronomers believe that the visible universe is pretty much the same from place to place. This means that the earth is not in any special location in the universe. If we found ourselves on some distant planet out at the visible edge, the universe would look the same from way out there as it does from way over here. This means that the universe just goes on and on in all directions. No matter where you are in the universe, when you look out at the stars, it appears that you are in the center.

The distance from edge to edge of the visible universe is about thirty billion light years. This is certainly a huge distance, but not infinite. Infinity is infinitely larger than this.

We think of God, the I AM, as infinite creative energy which has never changed, and will never change, in intention, responsiveness, character, or purpose. We can think this because that is what God is. Infinite intelligence. Infinite creative energy.

For I am the LORD, I change not... – Malachi 3:6

Infinite intelligence is a form of energy, and is one way to visualize God. Infinite Intelligence means that all of what we know as knowledge today has always been here. Not just that, but all the knowledge which ever will be known is also already here, in Infinite Intelligence. The total amount of knowledge is unchanged over time. There is no end to it! It only appears that new things have been discovered. We discover this "new" knowledge a little at a time, as it is revealed to us, but this new information has always been available to us. New knowledge is a small part of the endless reservoir of knowledge contained in Infinite Intelligence. All of the elements needed to make an electric car have always been here. All that was needed was the dream, the vision of the finished car, the idea of how the pieces could be produced and assembled, along with the will to do it. All that humans have created throughout history began with ideas, with thought energy. That energy, that knowledge, has always been.

Now are we sure that thou knowest all things... – John 16:30

Everywhere

Embrace infinity, for it is part of you. It lives within your creative mind.

Jesus said unto them, Verily, verily, I say unto you, Before Abraham was, I am. – John 8:58

God, Infinite Intelligence, exists in all space and time. But what does that mean? This concept is impossible for us to grasp completely. We all have very limited experience with space and time. An experienced world traveler has only gone around an insignificant, tiny dot in the universe. The oldest person on earth has only lived a brief instant compared with endless time. Infinite Intelligence existed before anything and is one hundred percent present in all places. God exists forever. In all places and times.

Infinite time is given a special name. It is called Eternity.

We have a common experience concerning our place in time. We see the seasons change, the tides rise and fall. Plants sprout, grow, and eventually die and decay. Animals and people grow, age and pass away. It seems like a one-way street, extending infinitely into the future and the past, and we are stuck here in the present.

Think of this. We know we can imagine the future. If you have a goal that you really want, like a new car or house, you can visualize yourself actually owning that car or house. With a good imagination, you can clearly see your goal in the future. If you can see it in your mind, you can hold it in your hands and bring it back to the present.

You probably know people who dwell on the past. We may even describe someone as living in the past. To a person who lives in the past, that past is very real to them. They may even have conversations with old friends who are gone, talk about their grown children as if they were still kids, or pick up an old argument with someone they have not seen in years and is not present in the room. Although it only exists in their mind, their past is very real.

A few years ago, I was introduced to a college student who was the son of a friend of mine. To open a line of conversation with him, I decided to ask him about his grade level in his undergraduate experience. "What year are you in?"

He answered quickly, "2014. What year are you in?" Maybe I looked like I was living in the past.

We all have a sense that time is a continuum that only goes in one direction, but that is not true. We know that we can, in our thoughts, freely travel into the past or the future. We can even create memories of future events in our mind.

Imagine this:

Think about a dream vacation you would love to take. Maybe it is a trip to some exotic place that you have never visited, like Tahiti. Now take just a minute to imagine that you have already purchased the tickets for next Christmas, and you will actually be going there! Think how excited you are as the big day approaches. You have packed your tropical clothes, and you have a new pair of flip flops and a sun hat. When the day arrives, you lock the front door to your house, start up the car and drive to the airport. After standing in line at airport security, you finally get on the jet and, after many hours, you get off the plane and look around at your dream vacation island. Imagine the new things you see when you arrive, the people and colors, sounds and smells. The air is warm and humid, exotic. Winding through unfamiliar streets, the taxi ride to your five-star hotel is exciting. Your beautiful room is prepared for you. The view out the open windows is fabulous, with coconut palms, beautiful flowers, and a brilliant blue ocean. You walk out onto the veranda and smell the tropical air scented with the perfume of flowers. You are happy, exhausted, and feel like you could stay here forever.

Now realize, you are actually reading a book. But while you were reading the preceding paragraph, you were in a place in the future, and you can remember exactly what you saw and experienced there in your Tahiti dream vacation in the future. You just created a future memory. Every person has the ability to project themselves in their imagination into the future.

We also know that there are other times when we get a sense that the still, small voice in our mind is speaking to us from a future that we have not yet experienced. It may be the voice of opportunity giving you insight into the possibility of a move you could make in your life to become more successful. Or it may be a warning that you receive, which makes you more careful while you drive and helps you to avoid an accident. When that voice speaks, the best thing to do is listen and start to see that future unfolding.

In reality, time is multidimensional. It is not just a two-dimensional line on which we are stuck in a moment called the Present. Past, present and future are all parts of the same thing. Our bodies may in the present, but in our minds we can visit the past and the future. God, Infinite Intelligence, is uniformly present in all time.

> *I am Alpha and Omega, the beginning and the end, the first and the last.* – Revelation 22:13

God has existed and is entirely present, at every point in time; at the beginning of time, and at the end of time. God is equally one hundred percent in every moment, in all time. There is no place in time when God was young, and no time when He will be old. There is no place in time where God did not or will not exist. To get this idea across, Jesus called himself "I am." "Before Abraham was, I am."

And we are, each of us, a part of that Infinite Intelligence.

We describe God in many ways. God's infinite presence in time is only one aspect. There is also the presence of God, Infinite Intelligence, in the physical universe, in infinite space.

> *He stretcheth out the north over the empty place, and hangeth the earth upon nothing.* – Job 26:7

Infinity is larger than anything, vastly larger than the largest thing we can imagine. The largest number, or the longest period of time when compared to infinity, is exactly zero. This is a concept which we cannot get our minds around, no matter how hard we try. There is a mathematical formula for this:

$$X / \infty = 0$$

This equation says that no matter how large a number you choose for "X," infinity is so much larger that the number you choose is, by comparison, nothing.

God, Infinite Intelligence, is completely, one hundred percent present in all time and in all space. This quality that humans give to God is "omnipresent."

> *I am Alpha and Omega, the beginning and the ending, saith the Lord, which is, and which was, and which is to come, the Almighty.* – Revelation 1:8

To think of God as infinite is somehow comforting, because it means that there is an endless supply of the qualities of God, like love, compassion, knowledge and energy, all of which are available to us, every one of us, at all times. It's an endless resource, and this endless supply is not just in the world around us. It is also within us.

> *...the kingdom of God is within you.* – Luke 17:21

These are some of the most important words Jesus spoke when describing our relation to Infinite Intelligence. The kingdom of God is within each of us.

In your heart.

Often in the verses and text, you will see the word "heart" is used. This is not meant to be the group of muscles which work together to move blood through your body. The Greek word, cardia, καρδία, translated as "heart" even today, was used in ancient times to denote "the seat and center of all physical and spiritual life, the soul or mind, as it is the fountain and seat of the thoughts, passions, desires, appetites, affections, purposes, endeavors" (so in English: heart, inner person, etc.). This is what we would today call our subconscious mind, the emotional part of the mind, which is also the channel through which Infinite Intelligence can flow into us, to inspire us.

We say that God is omnipresent; completely present in all places, at all times. Not just a part of God over here and another part way over there in a distant galaxy. No. In all places, one hundred percent present, at all times. One hundred percent in me, one hundred percent in you, and also one hundred percent completely present within every human. He is one hundred percent in every cell of your body, in every wave in the ocean, and in every atom, every star, every galaxy. This is a great mystery, and not easy to wrap our minds around.

Not only is God present in an atom or a galaxy, but you and I each have the entirety of Infinite Intelligence within us! Every cell of your body has the same amount of Intelligence in it as there is in the entire universe. This truth comes from the very definition of omnipresent. This is important and powerful, and needs to be stated again.

The kingdom of God is within you.

All Powerful

Do not look outside for the kingdom. Look inside yourself, to the deepest place of your heart. There you will find infinite power and understanding, waiting for you, to welcome you home. The kingdom is within you.

> *And I heard as it were the voice of a great multitude, and as the voice of many waters, and as the voice of mighty thunderings, saying, Alleluia: for the Lord God omnipotent reigneth.* – Revelation 19:6

> *God that made the world and all things therein, seeing that he is Lord of heaven and earth, dwelleth not in temples made with hands.* – Acts 17:24

Infinite Intelligence fills all space and time. According to the creation story in Genesis, the entire universe, including all living things, came into being because of the energy of Infinite Intelligence. We see around us amazing diversity of life, the orderly working of the thousands of interconnected systems within every living thing, beauty and intricate detail in the natural world, from planets to molecules, patterns that are repeated with mathematical precision. These observations point many people toward the idea of a Creator, a designer who, by the power of thought, was able to bring all things into being.

> *All things were made by him; and without him was not any thing made that was made.* – John 1:3

In order to bring everything in the universe into being, this Creator, God, Infinite Intelligence, I AM, must be in possession of an infinite amount of energy, must be "all-powerful." The name given to this quality is omnipotent.

All Knowing

Remember there are no limits to knowing. The higher you fly, the farther you can see.

There are four terms which are commonly interchanged, assuming they mean the same thing. They are: learning, knowledge, intelligence and wisdom. But they are actually quite different.

There is a story of a country couple who saved their money to send their oldest son off to be the first in their family to go to college. The boy was bright, and majored in mathematics. He came home to visit at Christmas. The whole family was seated around the big kitchen table, eating Christmas dinner. The boy's dad asked, "What have you learnt in that there mathematical class?"

The oldest son was happy to tell him, "Dad, it's like a whole new language."

His father answered, "Say something in mathematical language."

His son thought for a moment, came up with the formula for the area of a circle, and said, "Pi R squared." His dad slammed both hands on the table and shouted, "That's what we're paying for? You ain't learnt nothing! Everyone knows that pie are round!"

What we usually call learning comes from one of three sources. One way to learn is from books or some other way of transmitting information from one person to another. An apprentice carpenter may learn by information from books, from a teacher of principles of construction, or by working side by side with a master or journeyman carpenter. Learning can come from reading reputable information on the internet. All of these methods will impart information. Regardless of the information imparted, the bottom line is: in order to gain from the information presented, the student or apprentice must study, memorize, repeat and apply the information, whether it is in the form of an oral exam or by demonstrating with hands and tools that the information has been learned, that it has become a part of who the person is.

The second source of learning is from life experience. This is "trial and error" learning. It is also called the School of Hard Knocks, since the learning part usually comes as a result of the "error" rather than the "trial." The school of life is an uncompromising, demanding and sometimes brutal teacher. A good student of life will weigh the possibilities, risks and potential benefits of several options before diving in and attempting the "trial." This helps to reduce possible errors. But errors are valuable, as long as health and body parts remain intact. The old saying says, "What doesn't kill you just makes you stronger." Because we remember the errors, often much more clearly than a lesson from a book or lecture, we learn from our mistakes. Errors make an impression on our minds. The lessons taught are applied, and we grow. Later, those same errors become the stuff of memories and tall tales repeated to friends, children and grandchildren.

> *Nathanial saith unto him, Whence knowest thou me? Jesus answered and said unto him, Before that Philip called thee, when thou wast under the fig tree, I saw thee.* – John 1:48

Infinite Intelligence, in the form of intuition or inspiration, is the third source of learning. All of the knowledge that has ever existed or ever will exist is already present in Infinite Intelligence. We only need to tap into Infinite Intelligence, into the mind of God, in order to gain a little portion of that knowledge. Sometimes it is readily available. At other times, we first need to understand that our knowledge is very limited, and open our hearts in meditation or prayer, ask for answers, and allow God to give to us the knowledge we need.

Intelligence has little to do with learning, knowledge or wisdom. Intelligence can be described as the ability to visualize relationships between objects or concepts, and to use that ability to generate solutions to problems or create new and useful combinations of things. When we use the term Infinite Intelligence, it means that all possible combinations of all objects or concepts that have ever existed or ever will exist are completely and perfectly known. There is nothing unknown to Infinite Intelligence.

In life, there is no problem which does not have many solutions. All possible solutions already exist in the library of Infinite Intelligence, including the solution which is the best for each individual circumstance.

The idea of many solutions to a problem may be an uncomfortable notion. We learned in grade school that two plus two equals four, and there was no alternate correct answer. Later, in basic algebra, we learn that if $X + 4 = 6$, then $X = 2$. Again, there is no other possibility. But in advanced math, this is not always true. For some problems in differential calculus, there are often several possible outcomes to solving a problem. First, there may be no solution. This occurs when the equation describes something which simply does not exist. The second possibility is that there may be two solutions, one of which exists in the real world and one that is "imaginary." A third possibility is that if a single solution can be found, it may be possible to generate an infinite number of correct solutions. This idea was a little disturbing to me at first. Either no solution, two solutions, or an infinite number of correct solutions? That thought is horribly non-intuitive! But it is in fact true, well known, and accepted by mathematicians.

This same idea is true concerning the problems that life throws at us. The "no solution" option happens when we imagine a future situation, like when you were sixteen and you dented your mom's car while you were out with friends. In your mind you go through all of the turmoil of confessing what happened, imagine your mom's reaction, see no possible solution to the problem because you are overwhelmed with emotion and fear, and imagine the worst possible outcome. But that future is imaginary, with no solution because the reality does not exist. When the reality comes, it is never as impossible as you had imagined, and does contain a solution, even if the solution may be embarrassing and uncomfortable.

The idea of an infinite number of solutions happens all the time. When I make coffee in the morning, I go through pretty much the same routine. I count out the time to fill the pan with water, grind the beans for eight seconds, let the coffee steep for at least three minutes, and so on. When my wife makes coffee, her method is so different from mine that if I watch, it makes me anxious. But the coffee comes out just as good as the coffee I make, and I know that there are at least a dozen other methods that will make coffee just fine. My wife is no less intelligent than I am; maybe more so. She sees a different solution to the same problem, and her solution is just as valid as mine.

Learning and intelligence, however, are two very different things. I watch the weather. Not a weather channel or a weather app, but the weather outside. I have been a surfer for fifty years, and weather is very interesting to me. I know if the wind starts blowing from the south, there will usually be rain within twelve hours. It's not that I have any great intelligence, but I've watched this happen for decades, and rarely does it differ. I've learned that south winds are usually followed by rain. That is one kind of learning: the ability to make a prediction of an outcome based upon experience.

Another way of describing learning is being able to repeat facts. However, despite what they say in school, this is not true learning. Rather, it is the skill of being able to observe or take in information, list the information in your mind, and repeat the list. It is not really learning. Unfortunately, standardized tests and IQ evaluations measure exactly this kind of "learning," and evaluate the "intelligence" of a person by the ability to answer a series of questions on a standardized test.

True learning actually takes place in the following way: You take in information or data, group or organize it in your mind, then apply the information. You use it to create an idea. When you act upon the idea, results are produced. You observe the results. You analyze and evaluate the results. The evaluation of the results is the learning, because the evaluation can then be used to create a new or improved idea. This learning cycle becomes a self-perpetuating loop, continuously generating new ideas and more learning.

Creative intelligence comes directly from Infinite Intelligence. It is usually called "inspiration," and it can be used in coordination with the learning described above to apply what is learned; to create something that is an improvement on an existing concept, or to create an altogether new concept. Applying what is learned is called inductive reasoning, or taking several ideas then putting them together to form a new or larger idea. True creative intelligence involves receiving new information directly from Infinite Intelligence which was not known prior to receiving it. This is called inspiration, defined literally as "breathing in," the inflow of air or spirit, which brings a glimpse of understanding about something which is fundamentally true.

There are many words that describe intelligence. People are called book smart, canny, clever, genius. We admire people with common sense, and also people who can explain abstract concepts in a way that is understandable in common terms. We have icons of intelligence who are recognized by the whole world. People like Albert Einstein, the Dali Lama and Stephen Hawking are widely regarded as people with great intelligence. They have revealed things about how the universe works which was not generally known, and for the most part have been able to explain them in terms that most people can comprehend. Not many people have this gift.

Jesus was an expert at explaining things simply. He talked about the Infinite Intelligence of God in a way that common people have been able to understand for two thousand years. He also knew how to phrase things or give examples by telling stories so the underlying truth would be evident to common people, but remain a mystery to those who had spent years "learning" about religious rules and laws.

> ...thou hast hid these things from the wise and prudent, and hast revealed them unto babes. – Luke 10:21

Knowledge, as we use the term today, is really nothing more than the accumulation of information and the ability to recall it. The world is full of people with plenty of knowledge, but little intelligence. These people can recite facts, but have no idea how to repair a leaky faucet. There is nothing wrong with knowledge, but in order for it to be really useful, it must be mixed with creative intelligence. When that happens, problems can be solved, goals can be achieved, and new worlds of possibility can open up.

> In whom are hid all the treasures of wisdom and knowledge.
> – Colossians 2:3

Wisdom is a quality of character to which we all aspire. It encompasses learning, knowledge, and intelligence, but it also includes other characteristics which lift it above the other three. Some of these other characteristics are justice, ethics, and the incisive ability to cut through the superficial and get to the core truth of any situation, problem or disagreement. A person with wisdom looks at the effect and clearly understands the cause. Wisdom has a quality of spirit that is not included in merely learning or possessing knowledge.

One thing should be clarified. There is a difference between having knowledge and knowing something. Having knowledge really is an objective state of possessing information. A person with knowledge has in her or his mind specific facts which can be used to make a comparison, or an evaluation of a problem which needs to be solved. On the other hand, knowing something infers a deeper understanding, not only of facts, but of the underlying relation between facts and the emotions or motivations associated with the facts, or the interconnections between what appear to be isolated facts.

> *God is greater than our heart, and knoweth all things.*
> – I John 3:20

Wisdom has the additional element of intuition. A person with wisdom will hear not only spoken words, but the feelings, reasons and truth behind the words, and weigh all of the factors, said and unsaid, before proposing any opinion or solution.

> *Wisdom is the principal thing; therefore get wisdom: and with all thy getting get understanding.* – Proverbs 4:7

We know that the amount of knowledge accumulated by humans is increasing at a faster and faster rate every year. Humans now have the ability to double the base of accumulated knowledge about every five years. In the next five years we will gain more information than we gained in all of the previous millennia since time began. But has all of this "knowledge" made us any more intelligent? Are we, as a community, any more insightful? Do we know any more about ourselves or can we make any better decisions?

It is true that we have more information, but we are no more intelligent than an Egyptian laborer in the time when the pyramids were being built. That laborer helped to solve problems. We have more information than ever before at our fingertips, but our innate ability to reason, solve problems and imagine in a creative way has not changed. Today a person has logic, just as the students of Aristotle had logic. The great leaders of the modern world are certainly not greater than Moses or Solomon. Some things have not changed through the ages.

God is Infinite Intelligence. All of the "knowledge" there ever was and ever will be already exists in Infinite Intelligence. Infinite Intelligence also contains all of the understanding about how humans think and feel and make decisions. According to the mathematical formula given above, the sum of everything we know or will ever know as the human community, compared to Infinite Intelligence, is exactly zero! It's humbling.

We call this quality of God omniscience: all knowing.

All of Infinite Intelligence is one hundred percent present equally, everywhere, at all times. The really amazing thing is that this Intelligence, this knowledge, is available to each one of us. That's because it is a part of the kingdom of heaven. It is within us.

God knows all things. Everything that can ever be known in the universe is already present in the mind of God, Infinite Intelligence. Since God is entirely present in all places at all times, including every atom of every cell of our body, then every cell of our body contains everything that can ever be known in the entire universe.

All of the information in the universe that has ever been and ever will be is entirely present in every part of the universe, right now. However, some of that information has changed in form over time. Two thousand years ago, messages were carried by hand. Almost two hundred years ago we had the telegraph. Today we have smart phones. The information needed to develop a smart phone has always been here, we just needed to discover the information to bring the smart phone into existence.

Leonardo da Vinci drew up plans for a kind of helicopter. He had information "ahead of his time" for the design of a flying machine which in his day could not be made to fly because necessary components like aluminum, jet engines and carbon fiber had not been discovered. His flying machine could not be made to fly using wood, iron and wool because it was just too heavy. But he had inspiration about the information.

Seeing Within: The Heart of the Matter

What lies behind us and what lies before us are small matters compared to what lies within us. – Ralph Waldo Emerson

...for the LORD seeth not as man seeth; for man looketh on the outward appearance, but the LORD looketh on the heart. – I Samuel 16.7

...your Father knoweth what things ye have need of, before ye ask him. – Matthew 6:8

Intuition is a gift. It is a part of Infinite Intelligence that many people have experienced. Intuition is much the same as knowing that something will happen before it happens, but it also has to do with knowing something about a person whom you have never met. Some people are much better at this type of "reading" than others.

And Jesus knowing their thoughts, said, Wherefore think ye evil in your hearts? – Matthew 9:4

We have all had that "gut" feeling about a person or a decision we are about to make, and usually that feeling is accurate. How many times have you told yourself, "I knew I should have (or shouldn't have) done/said that," or "I knew he wasn't an honest person" or whatever it may be. That is intuition.

There is a story, often called *The Woman at the Well*, about an encounter that Jesus had during his travels. The story is related in John 4:5-39.

Jesus sat on the side of a well in a town of Samaria while his friends went to the store to buy food. A woman came to get water from the well, and Jesus asked for a drink. They got into a discussion, and Jesus told her details about her personal life that He could only have known by intuition. The woman realized His intuitive nature and was convinced that Jesus possessed the gift of intuition, which she knew came from God.

In another incident, Jesus knew the thoughts that were in the minds of a group of people who were asking Him questions:

> *And immediately when Jesus perceived in his spirit that they so reasoned within themselves, he said unto them, Why reason ye these things in your hearts?* – Mark 2:6

Since intuition is a part of Infinite Intelligence, it is also available to every one of us. It is called a "gift," but in fact it is already within each of us, one of our intellectual factors, and it is like a physical muscle. Most of us have not developed this intellectual muscle. Intuition can be strengthened and made more sensitive. The secret to learning how to strengthen intuition is to learn about yourself. Make yourself aware of your own inner feelings and emotions, how you react to a person or a situation, and how you feel when you react. Be aware. As you become more aware of yourself, you will start to become more aware of others. When you see another person, be aware of that person. Focus your energy on that person, and allow yourself to open up to her or his energy. Let yourself feel what that person is feeling. Are they content? Frustrated? Short tempered? Insecure? Unfulfilled? Determined? There are thousands of qualities of character and even goals that every person radiates like a beacon to someone who is sensitive to their broadcast frequency. You can learn to develop this gift, but it takes an open mind and sensitivity. You must first be open to yourself, and then to others.

Seeing the Future

Behind, the past, what was, and is not to be.

Ahead, an open door of opportunity.

> *...for your Father knoweth what things ye have need of, before ye ask him.* – Matthew 6:8

Prescience means "knowing before." If you have ever had the feeling that you knew something was going to happen before it happened, that is prescience. If that has happened to you, it is because for a moment you were "outside" of time. Your mind was partly in the future. Often we live in the past and don't think much about it. However, when we "see" something from the future, it's a big deal. But God exists in all time equally. Past, present and future are all the same. "Alpha and Omega, the first and the last."

Our human concept of time and of being trapped in the present moment is imaginary. It is really just a concept that we have invented because of the way we interpret our world. We see living things around us "grow up", "grow old", deteriorate, and change, all related to this thing we call time. Remember that time is one of the qualities of the physical world which is fundamentally undefinable. To exist in all time equally seems impossible to us. But most of us have had experiences of prescience, and know a little about being able to exist in more than one moment at a time, like the example of the future memory described earlier.

In fact, modern quantum physics allows equal probability for material existence in the past, present and future, simultaneously. Our sense of time is really only an illusion based on the cycles we see in the natural world around us.

Today there are people who fraudulently claim to be able to see into the future. They have psychic hotlines, internet and television ads, and they fool people into parting with their money. There are also people who truly have visions of future events. This is not a new thing.

"Seeing" into the future is a special gift which has been around for thousands of years. It is a gift which is available to all types of people. There is the story of Joseph, recorded in *Genesis*, chapters 39-41. The story is fascinating, but a little too long to quote. The short version is this: Joseph had been sold by his brothers, and was in prison in Egypt. Pharaoh had experienced a disturbing dream and discovered that Joseph could interpret dreams. Joseph was brought before Pharaoh, who described the odd images of the dream. After hearing the dream, Joseph told Pharaoh the significance of the images. He said there would be seven years of bountiful harvests followed by seven years of famine. Joseph was released from the prison cell and became the chief advisor to Pharaoh.

The interesting thing in this story was that the "seeing" came to Pharaoh, not to Joseph. Pharaoh did not worship in the Hebrew tradition, but he was able to see images of his world fourteen years into the future. Because of Joseph's interpretation, Pharaoh could help Egypt prepare for the years of famine that he had foreseen.

In the *Revelation of John,* the entire book is a vision into the future. It is full of odd images and graphic descriptions, but is considered a book of prescience, foreknowing. It is a book that has puzzled theologians for millennia, and is not clearly understood.

> *And now I have told you before it come to pass, that, when it is come to pass, ye might believe. –* John 14:29

Jesus also had this gift of prescience, since it is a part of Infinite Intelligence, part of the nature of God. He saw into the future and could tell his followers things that were going to happen.

> *And as they sat and did eat, Jesus said, Verily I say unto you, One of you which eateth with me shall betray me. –* Mark 14:18

The Kingdom of Heaven is Within You

Under an artesian spring, a bowl
Always emptying, always full
The secret of the water of life

I visited a historical site years ago, where early American explorers had established a settlement to survive a winter in the wilderness. The fort was built on the site of an artesian spring to ensure a constant pure water supply for the company. When I saw the spring, it fascinated me. It was bubbling out of the ground, still flowing nearly two hundred years after the day it was discovered.

But more than the flowing of the spring, something else drew me in like a magnet and touched a place deep in my heart. The spring had been made to flow into a circular, stone bowl, which flowed out of a spout built into the rim like two tiny waterfalls. The first stream filled the bowl and allowed someone to dip a cup into the bowl to get a drink of water. The second spout directed the overflow and could be used to slowly fill a larger container.

The bowl was what moved me. It was constantly being filled, and constantly pouring out. I had heard this paradox before. Always emptying, always full. I had thought about this paradox, but never knew how it could be possible, yet here it was right in front of me. Quietly bubbling with its watery sounds, this little clear artesian spring told me of a great truth. We all have the opportunity to be like that stone bowl. The spiritual energy of Infinite Intelligence is constantly flowing into us. We can be a vessel, a bowl, into which spiritual energy flows and fills us to the brim. The energy flows into us, through us, out to the world around us. From God, through us, to others. A great truth.

God is infinite, omnipotent, omniscient and omnipresent, entirely one hundred percent present in all places, at all times. This means that Infinite Intelligence is entirely present in every cell of our bodies, and also entirely present in the farthest edges of the universe. It's mind-boggling. We can visualize God out there in space, filling the universe more easily than we can visualize God confined within the walls of a microscopic cell. But, biologically, we know that in every cell of our body there is DNA which contains all the genetic information needed to completely reproduce our entire body exactly as it was when our body was first formed. Every cell – every muscle, bone and brain cell – contains God, one hundred percent. Nothing is missing. This omnipresent God is everywhere, all the time. Jesus explained it concisely:

> *Neither shall they say, Lo here! or, lo there! for, behold, the kingdom of God is within you.* – Luke 17:21

It's not just a part of the vastness of Infinite Intelligence. The whole kingdom, all of the energy and power of the entire universe, all of the knowledge of Infinite Intelligence, is within you right now, in this very moment.

> *I have said, Ye are gods; and all of you are children of the most High.* – Psalm 82:8

> *Jesus answered them, Is it not written in your law, I said, Ye are gods? If he called them gods, unto whom the word of God came, and the scripture cannot be broken...* – John 10:34-35

In every one of us, the creative energy of the entire universe dwells. There is no limit to what we have available to us! Jesus quoted King David when he said, "Ye are gods."

It can't be said any more plainly than that. We are gods. We are conscious creators. We each have within us access to the same power, energy, understanding and prosperity that created and maintains the universe. All we have to do is tap into it.

PART TWO:
THE PHYSICAL LAWS OF NATURE

Fundamentally Undefinable

Physicists study the natural world and base their knowledge on experimental data. This involves measurement of many kinds. From the data, general rules or laws about how the world works are proposed. As more information is gathered, the laws sometimes need to be changed to fit all of the data. Application of the laws will allow accurate prediction about how things will behave in the real world. It is the application of these laws that have allowed humans to build passenger jets, huge bridges, and rockets that can take people to the moon and return them safely to earth.

There are a few simple properties of nature that form the basis of all of the measurements and physical laws. These simple or "fundamental" properties are time, mass, distance and electric charge. Let's look at each of these very briefly.

We all have a good idea of how time flows. It flows one way and we are always stuck in the present. We are good at measuring time by dividing it up into smaller and smaller parts. There are years, days, hours, seconds, milliseconds, and so on. Time can be divided up into units that we all agree upon. The approximate length of the year and the day are determined by nature, although they vary slightly. Clocks and stopwatches can measure time accurately. Thousands of years ago the twenty-four hour day was established arbitrarily. The minute and second were also arbitrary units, just agreed upon by people in powerful positions.

But what is time, exactly? What is it that is apparently flowing in one direction? If we try to define it, the definition eludes us. Time is something that we inherently know, but cannot define. No one can. The Oxford dictionary even struggles to define time as "The indefinite continued progress of existence and events…" The term "progress" implies time, and you can't use time to define time! That's called a circular definition.

Then there is the subject of mass. What is that, exactly? Mass is defined as a property of matter. We say matter is anything that has mass and takes up space. So again, we haven't really defined anything. Circular definitions don't work in physics. Everyone knows that there is more of something in a heavy lead weight than in a Styrofoam ball, but what is it? Mass cannot be clearly defined.

How about distance? This is another thing about which we have an intuitive understanding, like how far apart two things are. But the term "apart" implies distance, and we are stuck again. Let's divide it up into little parts. Inches, meters, millimeters, miles, angstroms… the list goes on and on. Even the basic unit of the foot was defined as the length of some ancient king's foot, and the meter was defined in the 1700's as one ten millionth of the distance between the equator and the North Pole. In the end we are no closer to a concrete definition of the concept of distance than when we started.

Last, consider the concept of electric charge. We think there are two kinds, called positive and negative, and there is a smallest fundamental unit of charge, which is the charge on an electron. Flow of electric charge can be measured in units called amperes, or amps. Effects of moving magnetic fields on electric charges produces the "electricity" in our lights and motors, but no attempt is made by physicists to define exactly "what" electric charge is.

Electrons were once thought of as very tiny particles, like a super microscopic grain of sand, but that thought has changed drastically. Electrons are now called "point charges" with no physical size at all, only electric charge. In short, the electron is really only energy. Electrons appear to move in a very unpredictable way and randomly pop in and out of the physical universe. We'll look more closely at this in a moment.

The most important fact is, the basic units of physics cannot be defined, even though they can be measured. In fact, physicists don't even try to define them, but instead put them in a special category, which is called fundamentally undefinable!

> *O the depth of the riches both of the wisdom and knowledge of God! how unsearchable are his judgments, and his ways past finding out!* – Romans 11:33

Here's one example. Energy is defined as the ability to do work. Work is defined as a force moving through a distance. Force is defined by how a mass is accelerated. Acceleration is change in velocity in a given time. And velocity is distance travelled in a given time.

Wait a minute! Energy is apparently defined in clear terms, but in fact it is made up of mass, distance and time, all of which are fundamentally undefinable. No wonder we had problems understanding physics in high school!

The point is, science is based on things like mass, distance, time, and electric charge, which we do not even try to define, but which we know are real. At least, we think they are real. The fact that some things are fundamentally undefinable does not bother physicists. Fundamentally undefinable properties are the basis for defining all other properties that we measure. Scientific knowledge has come a long way by building on this foundation. Most modern technology has been created by knowledge and application of physical principles. Scientists know that some things cannot be defined, but this does not prevent scientists from measuring, learning and applying what is measured. Our understanding of the natural world is, after all, intuitive. Fundamentally undefinable properties cannot be described using precise physical terms. Instead, we need to draw upon our feelings and intuition. We need to resort to something more conceptual, more nonphysical, more "spiritual." We need to discuss the real basic concepts of science by using more spiritual terms, like faith and belief.

Action and Reaction: The Third Law of Motion

Isaac Newton was the most outstanding scientific genius of his day. In the late 1600s he invented the branch of mathematics that today we call calculus so he could accurately describe the orbits of planets around the sun. He developed the equation that describes attraction between any two or more objects, which we still call Newton's Law of Gravity. He also developed three laws of motion that comprise the foundation of what is called classical physics.

Newton's Third Law of Motion is well known and states simply: for action there is an equal and opposite reaction. It is sometimes called, in more broad applications, the Law of Cause and Effect. This principle explains, for instance, why a canoe glides forward when someone paddles. The force applied as the paddle moves backwards through the water propels the canoe in the forward direction.

Newton's Third Law can be used to calculate forces on simple machines like levers and pulleys. It is used to describe how airplanes fly or how a hammer drives a nail into wood, along with hundreds of other processes in the physical world. If you push down on a lever, something on the other end moves up. By pulling down on a chain attached to a pulley, you can lift a car engine with one hand. When a rocket engine burns fuel, the force of the burning gases pushes on the front of the engine and the engine pushes back, propelling the rocket forward. If I push with all my strength on a brick wall, the brick wall pushes back with the same force, and all I accomplish is getting tired. This is the law of equal and opposite forces. In both the physical world and in the spiritual, this is a law. It cannot be changed or ignored. It has been proven to be true in the physical world for over three hundred years, and is the basis of most engineering. In the nonphysical world it is understood intuitively, and will be discussed later.

Another Law, the first Law of Motion, is worth mentioning. It says that a moving object will continue moving in a straight line at a constant speed unless it is acted upon by an outside force. This is called the Law of Inertia. It also says that if an object is "at rest" (not already moving), it will remain at rest until an outside force makes it move. To get something to change requires force. Try moving a piano! Anyone who has worked with a stubborn animal (or human!) is well aware of this law.

There is one other Law of Motion, but this is not intended to be a physics class.

Conservation of Energy
Energy, Matter and Space

Another one of the fundamental laws of nature says that energy is never created nor destroyed. This Law is also called the Law of Conservation of Energy, or the First Law of Thermodynamics. This could also be referred to as "Energy IS," because the total amount of energy in the universe has been constant since the beginning. The nature of energy is change. It is constantly changing in form or moving from one place to another, but the total amount of energy does not change. The Law of Conservation of Energy says that energy cannot be created nor destroyed in any isolated or "closed" system, but it can change form. A "closed system" is a system from which nothing can be taken and to which nothing can be added.

In a laboratory, this "closed system" is created for measurements of energy. For example, my chemistry students performed a lab experiment to measure the energy contained in a roasted peanut, in heat units called calories. This was done by sticking the peanut on a long needle, starting to burn it using a Bunsen burner, then heating water by placing the burning peanut under a beaker of water. To make this a "closed" system, Styrofoam insulation was used to prevent heat loss around the burner and the beaker of water. After the peanut had finished burning, the change in temperature of the water was measured. The students obtained results for the calorie content of the peanut and compared their results to the value printed on the can of peanuts. Afterwards, the class shared the remaining peanuts in the can.

On a much larger scale, the universe is a "closed" system. Energy cannot come in from somewhere else and energy cannot escape. But it can change. Not only can energy change, but it is constantly changing form. Change is the nature of energy. In another section, we will refer to this as Perpetual Transmutation of Energy.

Take, for example, something that represents a simple change in energy, like a ball that is tossed straight up into the air. It starts by moving upward fast. It quickly slows as it rises, comes to a stop for an instant at the top of its flight, and returns back down, moving faster as it falls. This is a simple transformation of energy from what is called kinetic energy (or energy of motion) to potential energy, or energy that is stored because of the ball's height, and back to kinetic energy as it falls.

Another simple transmutation of energy occurs when you rub your hands together on a cold day. Rubbing your hands is energy of motion. Friction between your hands changes some of the energy of motion into heat, and you can use that heat to warm up your hands.

There are more complicated energy transmutations in our everyday life. The list of changes sounds a little like the children's rhyme, *The House that Jack Built*. You step on the accelerator of your gas-powered car. The accelerator pedal is a small lever which activates a throttle. The throttle causes more fuel to flow. The fuel inside the engine's cylinder explodes, producing pressure that pushes the piston, which turns other shafts and gears, and finally turns the wheels. Heat is produced by the initial explosion. More heat is produced as a result of friction in the cylinder and in the turning of all of the shafts, gears and wheels. Most of the chemical energy which was originally in the gasoline is changed into heat. This heat is released into the air around the car, but a fraction of the energy is converted into the forward movement of your car. In all of the changes, the total energy in the gasoline is converted or transmuted into some other form of energy, and the total amount of energy is conserved.

When you step on the brakes of your car, the energy of the speed of the car is reduced and it slows down. Much of the "lost" energy of the speed goes into the brakes and shows up as heat. Thousands and thousands of experiments over the past two hundred years have shown that the total amount of energy is always conserved in any reaction or change. Energy can change form, often in multiple or subtle ways, but the total energy before and after any change is always the same. The entire amount of energy that is in the universe today is exactly the same amount that was here at the beginning. Nothing has been lost. There have been billions and gazillions of changes, but the total amount of energy stays the same.

Sometimes the change in form is more dramatic because matter can also change in form and convert directly into energy. We have all seen the equation made famous by Albert Einstein, which is usually written $E = mc^2$. You probably remember that this equation says that a small amount of mass can be converted into a very large amount of energy. More importantly, it says that energy and mass are really the same thing. It does not say that energy is created. That cannot happen. But it does say something more important, beyond the law of conservation of energy. It says that matter is energy, just in a different form. This is a very important concept, which bears repeating. Matter is energy.

The energy inside stars is produced by changing mass into energy, in the process of nuclear fusion. Stars are made mostly of hydrogen and helium. When four hydrogens combine to form one helium, some mass is converted into energy and produces the light and heat that a star gives off. The sun is constantly losing mass, as mass is converted into energy. In fact, the sun is losing about four million metric tons per second! Fortunately, the sun is very large. It is massive enough that it will last a few billion more years before it begins to run low on fuel.

Since the equation $E = mc^2$ is a mathematic formula, the parts can be rearranged and still be true. Think of what this rearranged equation means:

$$m = E/c^2$$

This new equation says that energy can also be changed into mass. It takes a large amount of energy to convert into a small amount of mass, but it can be done, and since there is an infinite amount of energy in the universe, there is plenty of energy to account for all of the matter that we see. Stars, gases, liquid, solids. Even thought. Everything is energy, and it is always conserved.

To give you an example of how much energy is contained in matter, let's look for just a moment at that number in Einstein's equation, "c squared." C is the speed of light. In US units, that speed is 186,000 miles per second. That number, squared, is huge. If one gram of matter (about 20 drops of water) was completely converted into energy, that amount of energy would be enough to power a city of one million people for two years!

So, what about "matter", that thing which the physicist calls mass? We have the old model of the atom that looks like a tiny solar system, with the nucleus at the center containing protons and neutrons, and electrons like little planets whirling around it. Although this model helps to explain things like chemical reactions, we know today that the model is not exactly accurate. Electrons do not move in neat little circles around the center, but rather buzz around the center more like bees around a beehive, and the entire atom is in a very high state of vibration.

Not only that, but the dimensions of the atom are really astounding. If the proton at the center of a hydrogen atom were blown up to be the size of a golf ball, the electron orbiting around it would be, on average, about 30 yards away, and be a dot too tiny and fuzzy to be seen. The atom is far more than 99% "empty" space (actually about 99.9999999%). Not only is the atom almost all "empty" space, the tiny bit of "matter" that makes up the nucleus, the heaviest part of the atom, is also almost all "empty" space too. If we divide the parts of the atom even smaller, every part is almost all "empty" space. You can imagine what the conclusion is. Matter is really empty space filled with energy in a special state of vibration. Our physical world only appears to have substance which we can touch.

> *He stretcheth out the north over the empty place, and hangeth the earth upon nothing.* – Job 26:7

At one time, the space between the stars and galaxies was considered to be empty, a complete vacuum devoid of anything other than an occasional proton or electron. It is true that there is very little matter in interstellar space, but the universe is full of surprises. Today, space is known to be filled with a form of energy called the Quantum Energy Flux, which is one of the highest forms of energy known, and closely linked to the energy of thought. Physicists have started to change their idea of empty space. Many physicists believe that "the 'vacuum' holds the key to a full understanding of nature," and that the vacuum actually contains huge amounts of untapped energy.

Energy cannot be created or destroyed, but it can change form.

Entropy: Expansion and Decay

Growth and change is a part of life. We see the changes: from a small seed to a huge tree producing fruit, or from a microscopic embryo to an adult. Living things grow. It's a part of what makes them living things. In order to grow in an orderly way, energy needs to be put in. A plant gets energy from the soil and from sunlight. An animal gets energy from eating plants or other animals. In both cases, energy which is taken in is changed into orderly growth, or maintenance and repair of the body. This same principle is true for all systems, not just living plants and animals. Energy is required to grow or to maintain a stable system. If no energy is put in, the system, whether it is a plant, an animal, or a society, deteriorates into a state of chaos. When an animal dies, the molecules that were once part of the animal's organized living system disconnect from each other in the process of decomposition, but the energy they contain is not lost. It changes form, and that energy becomes available for other living systems to utilize.

Remember that energy is never created or destroyed. It just changes form. The total amount of energy is a constant that never changes. The energy that is needed to maintain order and growth for a plant, animal or society has to come from somewhere. So where does the energy come from? It comes from the infinite energy reserve in the universe, from the hand of God, from Infinite Intelligence. And when the flow of energy into a system stops, the system must change into a state of lower energy. It must decompose. The energy that was stored in the living system can become available to new growing, living systems.

This principle is called the Law of Entropy. It is also called the Second Law of Thermodynamics.

The Law of Entropy states that energy naturally flows one way: from a point of higher energy to a point of lower energy. If we look at this in terms of heat, if you take an apple pie fresh out of the oven and place it on a rack, it will lose energy and cool down. The lost heat of the pie is not really lost, it is changed into energy that warms the kitchen slightly. If the pie is left long enough, it will eventually cool until it is the same temperature as the room.

The Law of Entropy does not end with pies cooling off. It also states that the energy of any system will naturally drop to its lowest or most random state unless energy is put into the system. The Law says that in any reaction, entropy (the degree of randomness) increases. Only if energy is put in, can the system gain energy. Another way of saying this is that a system left to itself will move from order to disorder, also called chaos.

A tree represents an orderly system of cells that make up the roots, trunk, limbs and leaves. As long as the tree is alive, it is constantly taking in water, nutrients and sunlight, and using this energy to grow in an orderly way to become the best tree it possibly can. When the tree dies, it begins to decay. The cells start to decompose, lose their orderly configuration, and change back into the chemicals the tree was made of. Eventually the tree changes back into soil, air and water. The same thing happens to all living systems once they stop taking in energy.

Since the natural state of the universe is expansion, the Law of Entropy states that when energy is no longer utilized to maintain growth, expansion and order cease. For each of us, if we are not expanding, we stop growing, and a state of disorder sets in.

Waves: Vibration and Frequency

In classical physics there is no single law of vibration, but there is a definition of vibration. Vibration is defined as any kind of cyclic repeating motion, like a clock pendulum, a bouncing spring, or a ringing bell. It is accepted that everything in the universe is in a state of vibration. To get to a real "Law of Vibration" we have to look at a newer kind of physics called quantum physics, which was first studied in the late 1880s as electricity and light became better understood. It has been well defined since then, and explains things that classical physics cannot. We will go through an overview of the basic ideas of quantum concepts after a brief look at some examples of vibrations in nature.

Everything in the physical world is in a state of constant vibration. Vibrations are repeated motion, either back and forth or circular. These vibrations come in many different forms, some of which are too tiny to see. Some are too fast to see. Others are so large and slow that they go unnoticed. Solids, liquids and gases are states of matter (energy) in different modes of vibration.

What we think of as "solid" matter comprises atoms which are held in what is called a lattice, keeping them pretty much in the same position, but they are constantly vibrating.

That lattice reminds me of a concert I attended when I was younger, where Ziggy Marley, the son of Bob Marley, was the headliner. The concert was in a fancy hall usually used for symphonic music and theater performances. Ziggy told the audience that we were not allowed to leave our reserved seat locations, but we could stand and dance. As soon as the band started playing, everyone stood up and started to dance, without leaving their assigned seats. We were like a solid! All vibrating at the same frequency, but not leaving our place in the lattice.

You now know that what is called a solid is actually almost entirely empty space. If that is true, why can't you poke your finger through a table? That is because of two things. First, even though they are vibrating, the atoms are in a fixed position with respect to the atoms next to them. Second, the electrons make a cloudy shell around the atoms that can't be penetrated. Think of it like a bicycle wheel. Close to the tire, the spokes are much farther apart than near the hub, and when the wheel is stopped you can stick your finger through almost anywhere you want. But if you get the wheel spinning really fast, you can't stick your finger through anywhere. Don't try this at home! You will injure yourself, and may lose a finger. The spinning spokes make a nearly impenetrable barrier. Electrons around an atom are like the spinning spokes. Try as you might, you just can't stick your finger through a solid.

In liquids, the atoms or molecules are free to move around each other without any of the restrictions of the solid, but the molecules all have an attraction for each other, which keeps the liquid confined to a container. We can see this attraction at the surface, in a phenomenon called surface tension, which makes water form beads on a window. Maybe you have seen an insect called a water skipper "walking" on the surface of a pond. That water skipper is taking advantage of surface tension.

Water molecules, like all matter and energy, are in a constant state of vibration. The higher the temperature of the water, the faster the rate of vibration. If you heat a pan of water, eventually it will start to boil as the vibration of the water molecules becomes fast enough to free them from the liquid state and they become free floating molecules called steam or water vapor.

It is interesting that the amount of energy needed to change water into steam is five hundred times greater than the energy needed to raise the temperature of water that last degree to the boiling point. We will talk more about this later.

Gases have an even higher rate of vibration, and very little attraction for other gas molecules. At room temperature, air molecules move about four hundred miles per hour. That is why if someone is making coffee in the kitchen, you can smell it in the bedroom only a short time after it has started to percolate.

You have probably seen a shaft of sunlight coming through a window into a room. Usually in that shaft of bright light you can see tiny dust particles floating in the air. To the naked eye, they appear to drift smoothly and a little aimlessly on the light drafts of air currents in the room. Seen up close and magnified by a microscope, their motion appears quite different. They jerk and jiggle around like they are bumping into other tiny somethings that can't be seen, and that is exactly what is happening. This is called Brownian movement. It is caused by the dust particles being hit by tiny, invisible molecules of nitrogen and oxygen, moving and vibrating at speeds high enough to bump the relatively giant dust particle out of its smooth drifting. This also happens in water.

We know that everything in the universe is in a state of constant movement. Any motion that repeats itself is called vibration, whether it is very slow or very fast. The earth in its orbit repeats its elliptical path once a year. That is, for us humans, relatively slow vibration. Many of the slow vibrations are also referred to as cycles or rhythms, which are discussed later.

Everything is in a state of vibration. Vibration always produces waves of one kind or another. You have all seen water on a lake, river or ocean. Water waves can be used as a good example of waves that everyone has seen. Let's take a little thought journey to another place.

Imagine this: You are on a weekend trip in early October to a peaceful setting in the mountains. You are taking a relaxing walk along the edge of a quiet lake. It is a clear, warm evening, and the sunset is beautiful. There is no wind, and the surface of the lake is like a mirror. Mountains and trees with their autumn colors on the far side of the lake are perfectly reflected in the surface, an upside-down image of the real thing. Lining the edge of the lake are small, flat, rounded stones, the kind they call "skipping stones" because if you throw them just right, they will skip over the surface of the water, sometimes five or six times. You pick up one of the stones, turning it in your fingers until it feels just right. Holding it along its curved edge, you walk to the edge of the lake, and with a quick flick of your wrist you throw the stone spinning low over the water. It hits flat and skips – one, two, three, four times before sinking out of sight. As you watch, rings form where each skip landed, and travel out in perfect circles along the glassy surface of the lake. The waves eventually get to the shore at your feet, making the water rise and fall slightly as each wave arrives.

Whether they are water waves that you can see, or invisible waves like sound or light, all waves have three properties in common. Those properties are speed, wavelength or frequency, and amplitude. The speed is determined by the material the waves travel through.

The wavelength is just the distance between one wave and the same point on the following wave. Frequency is the number of waves passing a point per second. An example of this is the "flow" of electricity in your house wiring. The waves of electricity flow at a frequency of sixty waves per second. You have probably heard the familiar "hum" of these waves of electricity in a motor or heater in your house, or coming from the fluorescent lights at the supermarket. For sound waves, as the frequency gets higher, the sound has a higher tone or pitch. For light waves, the frequency affects color. Red light has a lower frequency than blue.

The final property for our purpose is amplitude. Amplitude is a measure of the amount of energy carried by the waves. In water waves, higher amplitude means higher waves. In sound, higher amplitude means higher volume. In light, higher amplitude means brighter light. You can have dim or bright blue light. The only change is in the amount of energy, the amplitude.

Think of the microwave oven in your kitchen. It produces energy which vibrates at exactly the same rate or frequency as a water molecule and can stimulate water molecules to vibrate more rapidly and heat up. This is how a microwave oven heats a bowl of food, but does not heat the container. The food contains water molecules, but the container does not. Microwaves make the water molecules vibrate and get hotter. This makes the food get hotter.

To summarize, waves are energy coming from a vibrating source. They carry energy out from that source in all directions. The energy by the wave can be changed or transformed into a different form of energy. The effects of some waves can be received by our sensory factors. We have the ability to see, hear or feel some of the waves that carry communication, but not all of them. And there are only a few kinds of waves that you can actually see.

Now let's apply this idea of waves to ourselves.

Resonance and Harmony

The rainbow – what a marvelous sight! It changes nature into a great, vaulted cathedral, complete with the awe of unknown height, the sense of holy ground. Colors alive with their own inner light, the great soaring arch hanging impossibly perfect, sacred in the sky.

Everyone loves to see a beautiful sunset or a rainbow. We are also attracted to the ocean and to waterfalls, places that produce what is called "white noise," known for its relaxing and healing properties. Many people are drawn to storm watching, walking on the beach, or staring into a clear, blue, summer sky or the deep vastness of a starry night. What is it that attracts us to these things?

As a child I loved parades, especially when the marching band went by. There was a thrill when the big bass drum approached. I could feel the Boom! Boom! in my chest as it went by. The vibration of the sound of the drum made my whole body vibrate.

Later in life, as a teenager, I became enthralled with learning to play the guitar. My father gave me a vintage acoustic guitar which he had bought from a friend. I practiced in my bedroom for hours each day until my fingertips were blistered. Two things stand out in my memory from those early days with the guitar.

One was the feeling of holding the guitar while I played. I could feel the sound from inside the body of the guitar vibrate against my own body. It was as if I was filled with the sound. When I stopped playing, the sound would continue to echo inside me, the ghost of a sound, and I didn't want it to stop.

The second memory came from learning to tune the guitar. In order to create notes that were in harmony, the strings needed to be "in tune." If they weren't, the sound was unpleasant, like fingernails on a chalk board. That "sour note" sound is also called discord. There is a way to tune the strings by matching the sound of one string to the string next to it. A person with a good "ear" is able to tune the strings just by hearing the notes, but another way is to pluck one string while holding it at a higher note, which matches the tone of the string next to it. When the two strings are perfectly in tune, something magical happens. Plucking one string will start the second string vibrating. The vibration can actually be seen! This is called harmonic resonance. When the two strings are in tune, they each will vibrate at exactly the same frequency. Starting one string to vibrate by plucking it will induce vibration in the second string because they are in harmony.

The same thing can happen between two people. When they are both on the same "wavelength," they are in tune, in harmony, and vibrate at the same frequency. The energy of one person causes the other person to start vibrating at the same rate. When more people are together in harmony, a veritable orchestra is created. Most of us have been somewhere this has happened, whether at a lecture, a religious talk, a music concert or a sporting event. Minds vibrating at the same frequency produce far more energy than the sum of the individuals could produce, through harmonic resonance. In wave physics, this is called wave superpositioning. Waves that are "in sync" add to each other to create more power than either wave has alone.

Waves vibrating in harmony are the secret to how your cell phone, television or radio works. When you tune your radio to a particular frequency, like 105.0, you are setting the receiving frequency inside the radio, and it will resonate with the frequency of 105.0. You cannot pick up 105.0 by tuning to any other frequency. If 105.0 is rock music, 105.2 may be a talk show. The signal coming from the broadcasting studio that is sent out at 105.0 can only be picked up by a radio receiver tuned to exactly the same frequency.

When you turn on the television and select a channel, you are selecting a frequency, and the same principle applies. The only difference is that the television signal uses a wider frequency band, so the sound and video can be sent separately, using frequencies which are only slightly different.

When you enter your friend's phone number on your cell phone, you are actually entering the frequency of the phone you are trying to call. There are an infinite number of frequencies for radio, television and cell phones, just like there are an infinite number of discrete colors in the rainbow.

When we see a rainbow, sunset, or a beautiful waterfall, something within our being resonates with the frequencies of the colors, sounds or movement, and it makes us aware at a deep level of the harmony that connects our spirit with the creative energy and harmony of nature.

Communication by Vibration

The heavens declare the glory of God; and the firmament sheweth his handiwork. Day unto day uttereth speech, and night unto night sheweth knowledge. There is no speech nor language, where their voice is not heard. Their line is gone out through all the earth, and their words to the end of the world... – Psalm 19:1-6

Communication is one of the most remarkable things in the universe. It is easy to assume that communication is an activity that is carried on by humans only, but just a little thought will make anyone realize that communication is more the rule in the natural world than the exception. All animals communicate, either with one another or by receiving meaningful information from their surroundings that they can interpret to help sustain their life. They get food or escape being eaten by correctly interpreting stimuli coming into their senses all the time. Social insects like ants and bees have well developed communication skills and use them to defend the colony, inform the group about food sources, or carry out the complex duties needed to keep the colony healthy.

Even body cells communicate with each other. That's how our bodies successfully heal from a cut or get rid of a viral infection. This communication between cells has been known to science since 1894, and is called chemotaxis. Cells in need send out a chemical signal and actually attract to themselves exactly the kind of healing cells they need. Communication is also used to keep body cells in order, contributing to the health of the whole body. Cancer cells are really nothing more than body cells which are not in communication with the other cells. They do not conform to the "row and column" order of normal cells, and do not recognize the reproduction or the manufacture of new cells as being a function given only to certain specialized cells. So they wander around the body, reproduce on their own, do not contribute to the system, and reduce the body's ability to function in a healthy way.

Communication has also been shown to take place even down to the fundamental particles and energy that make up atoms. This will be discussed later.

All communication is carried by waves of one kind or another.

Sound

Sound is energy from vibrations, like a voice, the strings of a cello, a motorcycle engine or a roll of thunder. The energy of the vibrating source is carried from the source of the sound in waves called pressure waves, and travels quickly though air, water or even solids. In air, the speed of sound is about 750 miles per hour. When you are talking with someone across the kitchen table, that speed is plenty fast enough to make the conversation flow normally.

The rate at which waves pass by a point is called the frequency. When a fast motorcycle speeds by, the sound is at a higher frequency as it approaches and lower frequency after it passes by. This is because of the speed of the motorcycle.

He that hath ears to hear, let him hear. – Matthew 11:5, Mark 4:9

When you see a flash of lightning, you know that the roll of thunder will start a few seconds later. The time it takes before you hear the thunder is related to how far away the bolt of lightning was. This is because light travels almost a million times faster than sound, so the flash of lightning appears almost immediately, no matter how far away you are, while the sound of the thunder comes by at the slow rate of only 750 miles per hour. It takes almost five seconds for the sound of the thunder to travel one mile. When you see the flash and start counting, one one thousand, two one thousand… for every count of five, the lightning is an additional mile away. The time between the flash and the thunder communicates information about distance to your brain.

Musical instruments produce sound waves. A lower vibrational frequency results in sound of a lower pitch or tone. Higher frequency means higher pitch. Put them all together in a particular sequence with the instruments "in tune," and we have music, which can be used much like language to communicate ideas and emotions. If you close your eyes while instrumental music plays, your mind will start to produce images according to the emotions you feel as you listen. You can be carried away to another world in your mind by the communication, that connection of the composer and musicians to your mind.

Tone can also carry meaning in spoken language. Many languages are called tonal languages because the same word can have very different meanings, depending on the tone and inflection of the spoken word. In the Mandarin language the word "ma" with one inflection means "yes", with another inflection means "mother" and with still another inflection means "horse." Even in English, there are many ways to say, "I love your shoes." Depending on the tone, the meaning that is communicated could be anything from "I think your shoes are attractive, I would like to have a pair," to "I hate your shoes! They are the ugliest things I have ever seen!" Same words, different tone.

In the beginning was the Word, and the Word was with God, and the Word was God. – John 1:1

God is love. God is also communication from Infinite Intelligence to human intelligence. In order to be effective communication, our mind must be on the same wavelength, the same frequency, the same vibration, as that of Infinite Intelligence.

Language

Communication is a fundamental process of life. We understand spoken language where thoughts are represented and communicated as a sequence of sounds. None of those sounds alone has any meaning, but we have attached meaning to them. Communication also takes place through vibrations of light and thought.

Humans have developed language to a higher degree than other creatures on the earth. Animals certainly have ways of communicating through sound, body language, scent, touch, and other ways that we do not understand completely. But humans have taken communication to another level where we can read, write and discuss verbally abstract thoughts or technical information in a sophisticated way, through time and over vast distances outside the capability of animals.

Because of communication, we have the ability to share abstract concepts like self and Infinite Intelligence. We are also familiar with ideas like goals, vision and purpose. Our language is full of conceptual words like persistence, will, desire, imagination, success and abundance, to which we give significance and which we can apply profitably to our daily lives.

More deeply, we understand nonverbal communication. Hand signals, posture, the twinkle in someone's eye, all give us information that we can interpret. There is also the lack of eye contact, which may indicate dishonesty, or the "eye roll" that says "I can't believe you just said that!" or "right, Mom – like I would take out the garbage!"

We often have a feeling of being guided along the path of life by something non-physical. Call it spiritual guidance, conscience, the voice of God or angels, this communication between humans and non-physical energy has been known for millennia. We even have a name for this guidance. We call it the still, small voice. Although there are many references to God speaking in an audible voice to people such as Abraham, Samuel and Daniel, that particular term "still, small voice" appears only once in the Bible, in a verse written about 600 BCE.

> *And after the earthquake a fire; but the LORD was not in the fire: and after the fire a still small voice.* – I Kings 19:12

There is another reference to guidance by a voice, written about the same time, by the prophet Isaiah. This verse has particular significance to me, and comes to me often as I walk the path of my own life.

> *And thine ears shall hear a word behind thee, saying, This is the way, walk ye in it, when ye turn to the right hand, and when ye turn to the left.* – Isaiah 30:21

This experience is common to many people, in all times. Jesus, in his day, saw into the future, as well as into other lands, and referred to a group of people of other times and places who one day would have faith in the guidance of Infinite Intelligence:

And other sheep I have, which are not of this fold... and they shall hear my voice... – John 10:16

We can communicate through another method which is even more abstract than spoken language: the written word. Writing is nothing more than a series of marks to which we have attached meaning. We call the marks letters. Alone, they mean nothing, but we have learned to attach a sound and a meaning to the little marks. We convert a visual image into a letter, arrange the letters to form words, and put the words together to form an idea or paint a mental picture.

Chinese, Bengali and Arabic are three of the top five most spoken languages. For a person who has not learned these languages, it is impossible to read them. But for a person who is fluent, like the "English" (actually Roman) marks on this page, they each carry meaning and can be used to create ideas.

Those little marks, put together in just the right way, are some of the most powerful things in the human experience. I can sit in my chair today and read words written by Plato or Solomon, or transcribed from the teachings of Jesus, Buddha or Mohammed. When I read a book, I can see into the mind and times of the writer. I can understand his or her thinking, and feel life's struggles and emotions as he or she experienced them. It's absolute magic! Writing is a true time machine, which I can use to get clear communication from a person that has not been alive on this planet for thousands of years.

Light

And the light shineth in darkness; and the darkness comprehended it not. – John 1:5

Electronic communication has changed civilization. First there was telegraph, a series of clicks. Then there was radio and television. Radio, television and mobile phones all use a form of vibrating energy called electromagnetic radiation. Like a rainbow, which is also electromagnetic radiation, there is a spectrum from lower vibration to higher vibration. Radio and television waves are in the lower vibrational range, or lower frequency, Visible light, the familiar rainbow, is toward the middle. At the higher frequency range, also higher vibration, are microwaves and x-rays. But all of these waves are called electromagnetic radiation, because they are made of electric and magnetic fields, and they can all be used to carry communication.

Information from light also comes in the form of vibrations, carried by wave-particles called photons, that travel at the speed of light. This electromagnetic wave communication has dramatically affected how we interpret our environment.

Now we carry tiny communication devices that give us sound communication, written communication and video images, which are just an organized series of colored dots that change to give the illusion of motion. When you make a call on your cell phone, the number you enter activates a precise vibrational frequency which matches the exact frequency of the receiver, the person you are calling, and makes their phone ring. Communication with another person requires that both phones be on exactly the same frequency.

Starlight

When you look at the night sky, remember

The light of each star is for your eyes only

No one else receives exactly the same blessing as you

We are all stargazers. Every person from the dawn of time has been enraptured with the majesty of the night sky. But why?

When we look out on a clear night and see the thousands of glittering points of light, something deep within us is drawn to the surface. We see unfathomable depths and a profound, unexplainable knowing of infinity. But there is something else.

Think about this. What we see is for our eyes only, and no one else anywhere sees exactly the same light from each star that you see. Those tiny bits of energy that pass into your eyes do not go anywhere else, and what comes to your vision does not take away any of the beauty, grandeur or wonder that someone else receives. Not only that, but there is communication in that energy, from every star.

Astronomy has been called the purest of the sciences because everything we know about stars we have learned without physical contact. We can only look at light. The light of every star completely fills its visible universe. By analyzing the light of stars, we know about their temperature, size, how far away they are, their chemical makeup, and even whether they have planets around them. This is a huge amount of information that we humans have gained by looking at stars with open, questioning minds.

Starlight gives us a physical picture of how things are in the nonphysical universe. Infinite Intelligence is energy which permeates all space and time, and that energy carries messages, communication that connects every one of us to everything else.

Just as stars are hidden during the light of day, they also go in and out of our awareness. But on a clear night, the most common phrases uttered when a person looks up is, "Look at all the stars! It seems like you could reach out and touch them!" And you can, because they touch you. With their light.

The Law of Attraction

There are two parts to this physical law, so it is often referred to as the Law of Attraction and Repulsion. Let's look at a few examples.

Take two magnets. The north pole of one magnet is attracted to the south pole of a second magnet. If you try to bring the north pole of one magnet close to the north pole of a second magnet, it gets harder and harder to bring them together the closer the two magnets get to each other. We say that "like" or similar poles repel, and opposite poles attract. South repels south. If you have ever used a compass, you know that the "north" pointing end of the needle always points toward the north magnetic pole of the earth. This was known thousands of years ago in the early days of navigating in the ocean. A sliver of a mineral called lodestone, which is high in iron and is also magnetic, was suspended near the tiller, where the helmsman steered the boat, so even in cloudy weather the helmsman had a method of determining direction on the open sea. This method still works well today in most parts of the world, but we know now that the "north" pointing end of the needle is actually the "south" pole of the magnet.

In the case of electrical charges, a similar rule applies. Opposite charges attract, and like charges repel. But unlike magnets, the opposite charges are not called north and south, they are called positive and negative. Negative charges are attracted to positive charges, much like magnetic poles, and two positive charges repel each other. This principle is used to control how electricity flows through wires. If you imagine a AA battery, you may have noticed that one end has a "+" sign and the other end has a "-" sign. The ends are labeled so that when you put the battery into a device that needs batteries, electrons will flow in the correct direction through the tiny electrical circuits. If you try to put the battery in backwards, the electrical circuits may be damaged.

The law of attraction and repulsion is also the principle which causes electrons to travel though a vacuum in an x-ray machine or in an "old-fashioned" television picture tube. It is the magic behind every piece of modern electronic technology, from computers to GPS systems.

The law of attraction and repulsion between electrical charges is one of the fundamental principles which describe how atoms bond to make molecules and chemical compounds, even complicated molecules found in living things like amino acids, proteins and DNA. The Law of Attraction and Repulsion is one of the immutable laws of physics.

Another one of the laws dealing with attraction and repulsion is the law of gravity; derived by Isaac Newton and included in his most famous book of natural laws, The Principia, published in 1687. When we look at the law of gravity, there is a major difference between it and the laws dealing with electrical charge and magnetism.

For gravity, there is no gravitational repulsion. All objects are attracted to all other objects by the force of gravity. It does not matter how large or small the objects are, there is still a force of gravity between them. But the law says that the force of gravity is determined by the mass of the objects and how far apart they are. So an object with a lot of mass, like the earth, has a much larger force of gravity than a baseball. If you throw the baseball up into the air, it falls back down – or it appears to. Actually, the baseball is also attracting the earth to it, and the earth must move toward the ball, by law. But since the earth is so much more massive than the ball, it moves an unmeasurably small distance toward the ball as the ball falls.

Everything on the earth is affected by gravity. Gravity pulls everything as if the entire mass of the earth was concentrated at its center. That is why two mountains do not move toward each other. The force of gravity pulling them toward the center of the earth is much stronger than the force of gravity between the two mountains. This center-directed force also explains why the earth is a round sphere, and why the stars and planets are also spheres. All of the material that makes up the earth is drawn toward the center of the earth by gravity.

We use the force of gravity to define the direction we call "up," which really means "away from the center." If you asked a person in Australia and another person in England to point "up" they would point in opposite directions, but both of them would be pointing away from the center of the earth.

The Quantum World

All that we know about the universe comes to us in waves.

Everything is in a state of vibration. This law of physics extends down to particles much smaller than atoms, in a world governed by something called quantum physics.

Quantum physics forms the foundation for much of our modern technology, like fluorescent light bulbs, orange sodium street lamps, solar electric cells, LED lighting, and microcircuits used in computers and cell phones. One of the fundamental concepts in quantum physics is that everything in the universe vibrates, but quantum physics also contains some very non-intuitive ideas.

You know that there is no real substance called "matter" as we think of it in everyday terms. On the subatomic level, what we think of as particles, solid bits of something, are really made up of only energy that is vibrating in a wavelike manner, and it is this vibrating energy that gives the appearance of "matter." Even though we can measure things like the mass of these "particles," they do not really resemble a grain of sand or a marble. Everything, including all matter, is energy. Energy just is.

Whether it is an electron, atom or molecule, every kind of particle has wavelike or vibrational properties, as well as an energy field around it. Electrons have an electron field. Photons, particles of light, have a photon field. The same is true for all other particles smaller than atoms, with odd names like gluons, muons and bosons. Every known type of particle has its own type of field. The really strange and mind-blowing concept is that the field for each type of particle extends uniformly through all space without interfering with the fields of other types of particles. What appear to be actual particles can be thought of more like "wrinkles" in the field, places of concentrated local vibrations that manifest as "matter." The more physicists learn, the more the "fabric" of the universe takes on characteristics similar to Infinite Intelligence. Like God, the I AM, vibrational fields are uniformly present in all places at all times, and account for everything that exists as energy or matter in our universe.

In the quantum world where things get fuzzy and hard to pin down, the "fundamental frequency of vibration," the vibration called the Planck length, is unimaginably fast, trillions and trillions of vibrations per second. It is in this vibrational realm that we find thought vibration, so it's no wonder the energy of thought has not been accurately measured. Vibrating at this rate, this type of energy, like thought energy, can be transferred between particles or people instantaneously, regardless of how far apart they are. There have been many quantum physics experiments which have verified this instantaneous movement of energy using a known particle interaction called Quantum Entanglement.

We will not go into this in detail, but here is the essence. Remember: nature wants to maintain balance. Some subatomic particles have a quality called spin, and come in pairs. If the spin on one of the pair is reversed, its partner gets a "signal" to reverse spin, and reverses in response, keeping the spins balanced, even though nothing is done to directly affect the partner particle. This "signal" seems to be received instantaneously. Even if the distance between the particles is large enough that the "signal" has to travel faster than the speed of light to get to the partner, it still happens. You can search this out if you are interested in the details. While you are searching, look up the fascinating results of the "double slit" experiment and the Heisenberg uncertainty principle. Quantum physics holds many secrets about thought energy.

It has been demonstrated that the "empty space" between atoms, between planets, stars and galaxies, is filled with this highest form of energy, the Quantum Field. This energy is much more like the energy of thought than any of the physical forms of matter/energy. It is in a very high state of vibration, and is itself the medium through which thought communication travels from one person to another, or from any form of creation to any other form. It is this energy which attracts one person to another when they are both "on the same wavelength" or "in sync" with each other, each with a harmonic vibration. It is the feeling of being in love and of daydreaming. It is the essence of the blessing that we feel in prayer or meditation – communication with God.

Thought

In thought we come closest to knowing the mind of God.

The highest form of energy is thought energy, and it represents the highest form of communication because it can be used not only for communication between one person and another, but between Infinite Intelligence and the human mind. Thought energy travels at a speed which appears to be infinite. Since it is not a "physical" phenomenon, thought is not bound by the law of physics which states that physical matter cannot travel faster than the speed of light. Thought is an open channel of communication between God and humans.

The phenomenon of thought energy is not peculiar to humans. Experiments in the realm of quantum mechanics have shown that there is "communication" between subatomic particles, discussed above, which is instantaneous and does not decrease in strength with distance, like sound or light. This communication has been compared by physicists to the energy of thought. In addition, biochemistry has shown that cells can communicate with each other by electrical or chemical waves to initiate healing or to fight viral and bacterial invasion.

Regardless of the form of communication, information is carried on vibrational frequencies from one point to another. Our minds are engines for communication, and we have a driving impulse in our DNA to create order and meaning out of vibrational waves. The vibration of thought energy is our portal to Infinite Intelligence and enables us to communicate with, interact with, and benefit from the great storehouse of Infinite Intelligence.

Communication is a fundamental definition of life. As humans, we have developed it to a high level. We understand spoken language, where thoughts are represented and communicated as a sequence of meaningless sounds. We create meaning and order through the written word, tiny marks on a slate. We receive communication through vibrations of light waves, resulting in a whole spectrum, from appreciation of beauty in nature to interpreting the electromagnetic vibrations of our phone or television. Behind it all is the energy of thought. Thought by itself is capable of transmitting information and emotion from person to person, or between the mind of a person and the mind of Infinite Intelligence, the Source of all communication.

PART THREE:
SPIRITUAL LAWS OF THE UNIVERSE

Divine Oneness: I AM, Energy IS

We know that Energy, God, Infinite Intelligence, is evenly distributed everywhere in the universe and that, according to the laws governing quantum fields, every part of the universe has an intimate connection with every other part. This connection can be best described as communication of a form similar to thought. You have probably experienced this for yourself, if you think about it.

Imagine you are hiking with your best friend who is in front of you along a steep trail. Your friend suddenly trips and falls. You shout, "Are you OK?" They get up, and you are shocked see there is a nasty, bleeding gash on their knee. In that instant your body shudders. You "feel" the injury that you see on your friend's knee. The sensation in your body is very real, and it is a common response to seeing another person's injury.

In your own body, you know that every part of your body is connected to every other part. Not directly, like with muscles and bone, but there is a connection. When I was working as a home builder, one day I hit my thumb with a hammer and it hurt clear up to my elbow. It swelled and my thumbnail turned purple. I couldn't stop thinking about it and how much I didn't want to hit it again. At the time, I didn't understand the power of negative affirmations. A few hours later, I hit it again! It hurt clear up to my shoulder. That evening I had a headache from the pain, and even my ankle hurt. Although my elbow, shoulder and head were not touched in any way, there was a connection between my thumb and the rest of my body that was very real.

One connection between all parts of a person's body is the nervous system, with millions of connections between cells, tissue and other systems. Every part of a living body communicates with every other part.

The Law of Divine Oneness goes even deeper. Just as every cell in my body is intimately connected with every other cell, I am connected with every part of the entire universe. This is something that many people understand intuitively. When someone says, "I love being outside because I feel one with nature," they are expressing this truth. It is not hard to understand since even physics says that vibrations of the fields associated with the smallest known particles extend outward in all directions to fill the entire universe, and vibrations at one point in a field instantly transmit to all points in the field.

Infinite Intelligence is omnipresent; in all places at all times. Not just a little part over here and another part way over there in a distant galaxy. No. In all places, one hundred percent present, at all times. One hundred percent in me. One hundred percent in you. One hundred percent in every molecule of your body, in every wave in the ocean, and in every atom, every star, every galaxy. This is a great mystery, and not easy to wrap our minds around.

...the kingdom of God is within you. –Luke 17:21

This fundamental connection between all things in the universe can be illustrated another way. Imagine this:

You are at your favorite beach on a sunny, summer day. The water is pleasant, and you wade out knee-deep with an empty glass jar. Bending over, you dip the jar into the water. It fills almost instantly. You lift the jar, look into the water, and then taste the water. It is salty! The salinity, density and mineral content of the water in your jar is exactly the same as the ocean water. In fact, there is no difference between the water in the jar and the water in the ocean. If you poured your jar of water back into the ocean, there would be no way to tell which was your water and which was the ocean because it's exactly the same.

Every one of us has a little "jar of ocean water" within us. What is within us is exactly the same as what makes up the whole universe. This analogy helps us to understand that what is inside us, our thought, mind and spirit, is part of a much larger whole. But this analogy doesn't tell the whole story, it's only a tiny glimpse of the whole truth. We do not contain just a little portion of Infinite Intelligence, we contain ALL of Infinite Intelligence because God is entirely one hundred percent present in all places at all times. Because of this, we have available to us infinite resources, infinite abundance, infinite knowledge. The kingdom of God is within you!

Think about the possibilities. We are all connected to one another, and all of us are connected to Infinite Intelligence. We have infinite resources available to us at all times.

This connection, this communication with Infinite Intelligence has been available to humans for centuries. In some people, this "spirit" has been powerful enough to be evident to everyone around. Take Daniel from the Old Testament, as an example. He was living in the kingdom of Babylonia, and was recommended as a person who could solve a problem that the king had. Daniel's gift of communication with God was evident even to those who did not adhere to the Hebrew teachings.

> *There is a man in thy kingdom, in whom is the spirit of the holy gods; ...light and understanding and wisdom, like the wisdom of the gods, was found in him... – Daniel 5:1*

We are God's highest form of creation. In fact,

> *...God said, Let us make man in our image, after our likeness... So God created   man in his own image, in the image of God created he him; male and female created he them. And God blessed them... – Genesis 1:26-28*

We have been made in the image of God.

What is the image of God? Like many people, I grew up with the classic images of God. Is it true God looks like a human? No. God is spirit, infinite, omnipresent, and the creative power of the universe. This does not sound like a human, but all humans do have a spiritual side. They are by nature creative. "...God created..." Deep within the heart of every person is the desire to love and be loved, whether it is expressed or not. "...God is love..." And even though there are some people who seem to look only on the negative side of everything (we all know this "someone"), it is part of our nature, part of what makes us unified in our humanity, to look for the good in a situation. "...God saw that it was good..." In spite of the people who take and then take more, most people have in their nature the spirit of giving because for some reason giving just makes us feel better. "...it shall be given unto you; good measure, pressed down, and shaken together, and running over…" And we know a feeling of fullness of life when we wake up and go to sleep with a feeling of gratitude in our mind.

> *In every thing give thanks: for this is the will of God…*
> *– 1 Thessalonians 5:18*

Humans understand concepts like love, infinity, responsibility to care for other living things, eternity, and the spirit within us which does not die. We have the ability to choose. These are parts of what God is like. We are created in the image of God. We have been given the ability to create, love, choose, see the good, give, be aware, and have gratitude. All these qualities are part of the image of God.

In two other references, we find:

> *Jesus answered, My kingdom is not of this world… now is my kingdom not from hence. –* John 18:36

> *Neither shall they say, Lo here! or, lo there! for, behold, the kingdom of God is within you. –* Luke 17:21

These are some of the most powerfully affirmative words in history! We are made in the image of God, given God-like power, and blessed by God. The kingdom of God is within us. That kingdom is not of this world. We are one with the Creator, and we are one with all creation. David even said:

> *Ye are gods; and all of you are children of the most High.*
> *– Psalm 82:8*

When Jesus quoted David He said:

> *Is it not written in your law, I said, Ye are gods? If he called them gods, unto whom the word of God came, and the scripture cannot be broken… –* John 10:34-35

Humans have been given a great gift. We have the ability to understand our oneness with God, with each other, and with everything in the universe.

Divine oneness.

Correspondence

As above, so below:

The principle of Correspondence is an overlying principle connecting the physical universe to the spiritual universe. Simply stated,

As above, so below; as within, so without.

> *Thy will be done in earth, as it is in heaven.* – Matthew 6:10

> *A good man out of the good treasure of his heart bringeth forth that which is good; and an evil man out of the evil treasure of his heart bringeth forth that which is evil: for of the abundance of the heart his mouth speaketh.* – Luke 6:45

There is a story about a waitress who served a cup of coffee to a patron from out of town. The customer started a conversation. "I'm thinking of moving here. You must see a lot of people. What are the people like in this town?"

"What are the people like in the town you are moving from?" the waitress asked.

"Oh, they are a bunch of liars and cheats. I could never get an honest answer from one of them."

The waitress didn't hesitate. "That's too bad! I think you'll find people are pretty much the same here."

The customer finished his coffee, thinking. On the way out, the customer said, "Thanks for the tip! I think I'd better look around for a different town."

Later in the day, a woman came in and ordered a glass of orange juice.

When the order came, she observed, "You look like a nice person. I'm getting transferred to the hospital here, and I wondered what the people here are like."

The waitress again asked, "What are the people like where you live now?"

"They are so friendly and helpful! I just love them, and hate to be leaving."

"Don't worry a bit," the waitress told her, "I think you'll find the people here are as nice as any you can meet."

The woman thanked her. "That makes me feel good about moving here."

What is inside us affects the world around us and the way we perceive it. Our perspective, in large measure, determines how we see the world. Change your view, and your view changes. The world around us, the people, weather, and challenges, are nothing more than a reflection of the world inside our thoughts. The old saying says: as within, so without. This is one part of the principle of Correspondence. Our definition of the world around us is a mirror of the world inside us.

> *For as he thinketh in his heart, so is he.* – Proverbs 23:7

> *A good man out of the good treasure of the heart bringeth forth good things: and an evil man out of the evil treasure bringeth forth evil things.* – Matthew 12:35

The other part of the law of correspondence is "as above, so below."

> *Thy kingdom come. Thy will be done, as in heaven, so in earth.*
> – Luke 11:2

All of the Natural laws have equivalent laws in the spiritual universe. This is the principle behind the parables told by Jesus. A parable is an earthly story with a spiritual meaning. The parables of Jesus are timeless, simple stories of everyday life that were familiar to people in ancient times and are still familiar today. But they are much more than entertaining stories with a human-interest value. They can be easily applied to personal growth by someone who is seeking to expand and improve their life because parables have a rich depth of meaning on the spiritual level, although not everyone understands parables. The people who "get" a parable are those who are seeking spiritual meaning in their lives. To most people they are just stories. Jesus knew this very well, and told His disciples:

> *...Unto you it is given to know the mysteries of the kingdom of God: but to others in parables; that seeing they might not see, and hearing they might not understand.* – Luke 8:10
>
> *That seeing they may see, and not perceive; and hearing they may hear, and not understand;* – Mark 4:12
>
> *And in them is fulfilled the prophecy of Esaias, which saith, By hearing ye shall hear, and shall not understand; and seeing ye shall see, and shall not perceive:* – Matthew 13:14

Jesus explained some of the parables to make the spiritual meaning clear, but others were told without explanation. One common theme of the explanations is: things which are true in everyday life are also true in the spiritual sense. As above, so below.

Perpetual Transmutation of Energy

Change is constant in the physical and spiritual universe. The natural law of conservation of energy states that energy cannot be created nor destroyed, but it can change form. This is called the Law of Perpetual Transmutation of Energy in the spiritual sense. Like the natural law, it says that the total amount of energy that was in the universe at the beginning of time is exactly the same amount of energy that is in the universe today. Nothing has been added, and nothing has been lost. The spiritual law only differs from the natural law in that the focus is on the continual change of energy from one form to another, and not so much on the fact that the total amount is unchanged. This is because change is a huge part of how the universe works.

This may seem like a paradox. Some readers may think, "Wait a minute! You said earlier that God does not change, now you say that change is in everything. How can that be?" Remember that the total amount of energy, knowledge, power, and wisdom has never changed and will never change. God, Infinite Intelligence, does not change in nature nor in the sum total of energy, and God does not change in intention or character. But energy is constantly changing in form. Change is the nature of energy. It is constantly transmuting or changing, whether by changing in form or moving from one place to another; from light to heat to motion to chemical change. Matter changes into energy and energy into matter. The number of changes going on simultaneously is infinite!

We often read or hear that some "new knowledge" has been "discovered." In fact, the reality is that knowledge has always been there. It is part of the character of Infinite Intelligence. The total sum of knowledge, of what is known, has been known and will be known, is the same now as it ever has been. The knowledge of the wheel has always been in the universe. Someone just had to have a mind which was seeking an answer about making work easier, to find an inspiration, to attract the idea of the wheel. He or she also had to be a person who took action, made a wheel or two, and attached them to a wooden box. The "new knowledge" came as thought energy to someone's open, seeking mind.

What we know today as advanced technology, like the cell phone or photovoltaics, is part of the sum of knowledge that has always been. We watch movies or old television episodes from the 1980s and laugh at the "cell phone" that is the size of a brick. In the near future, we will look back at today's phone and think that "it looks so old-fashioned compared to what we have today!" As new ideas are brought into being, our world changes, sometimes in dramatic ways, but the total energy and knowledge is unchanged.

Vibration

Nothing is stationary. Everything around us and within us is in a state of constant motion. Everything! This is true for the physical universe as well as the spiritual universe. "As above, so below."

Every atom and every molecule in your body has its own natural rhythm of vibration. Your body also has its own rate of vibration as a whole, which is not just the sum of all its parts. All the cells in your body communicate with each other. This is the only way your body can communicate nerve impulses to the brain, move muscles in reaction to stimuli, fight infections, or transfer nutrients and oxygen, and at the same time remove wastes. Because the cells that make up your body are parts of a unified whole, the normal, healthy vibratory state of your body is one of harmony. The vibrations of your cells are in harmony. This state of harmony is also called a state of "wellbeing." When you have an injury or an infection in your body, that part is not in complete harmony with the rest of your body. If you have an infection, your body is in fact fighting a foreign invader and you feel "out of sorts" or "off." If you have an injury, your whole body is in sympathy as it works to begin the healing process. You know if there is disharmony or discord in your body. You feel a need to rest, take a hot bath, eat or drink some type of healing food, tea or broth, and focus your mind on bringing your body back into harmony.

The energy produced by thought, whether it is conscious or subconscious, also vibrates at different frequencies (rates of vibration). Depending on the focus of your attention, your desires or your emotional state, your frequency of vibration will change. The energy produced by these different states can actually be photographed. You have probably heard about the phenomena called auras, which some people can see surrounding a person's body. Auras are also related to the vibrational state of the mind. If you are sad, depressed or apathetic, you say that you feel "down" because your frequency of vibration is low. You might even feel like your body is heavy and it is difficult to move a muscle. I know I have felt like that. It's like trying to run in a swimming pool! This state of vibration is also referred to as "negative." A person in a negative state of vibration may attract more negative energy to himself or herself.

If you are enthusiastic, excited, interested or otherwise "stoked", your rate of vibration, your frequency, is "high" or "positive." You might even feel like you are weightless or floating. The highest rates of vibration are achieved through love, sex, faith, prayer and enthusiasm. A common phrase that describes the feeling of infatuation is "I was swept off my feet!" and there is a good reason why it is called "falling in love," because the feeling of falling describes very well the high rate of vibration and the feeling of weightlessness, like the state of free falling. A feeling of renewed faith is said to "lift up" a person, and receiving good news makes you feel like you are flying. All of these descriptions ring true because raising the frequency of vibration puts your mental and thought energy into a frequency that brings you closer to the frequency of Infinite Intelligence. Your mind comes into closer harmony with the creative mind of God.

It has been shown that the human brain is a sending and receiving station for frequencies of vibration, that "brain waves share the fundamental constituents with acoustic and optic waves, including frequency and amplitude" (da Silva, F. L., Neural mechanisms underlying brain waves: from neural membranes to networks. *Electroencephalography and Clinical Neurophysiology*, Vol. 79, No. 2, 1991, pp81-93.). Almost everyone has experienced this in some way. When you talk with a good friend, you are "in tune" with them and cannot only communicate easily with them, but actually increase both of your energies by the communication. If you have ever been a member of a small group of people who think in harmony at the same level of vibration, as in a professional group brainstorming to solve a problem, a football team listening to an inspiring coach at half time, a prayer group related to any faith, or a group of creative thinkers coming up with new ideas for improving a community, school or some kind of new technology, you will know that this "mastermind" group not only feeds on the energy brought by each person, but actually raises the level of vibration of every person in the group. The mastermind principle increases the energy of the group far beyond the sum of the energies of each person. It is as if an unseen additional person is adding to the group. This fact has been known for centuries, and is used to great advantage. It is the principle of the "prayer groups" in which people of many faiths take part.

> *For where two or three are gathered together in my name, there am I in the midst of them.* – Matthew 18:20

When the vibrational frequency of a group is "in tune" and positive, the additional energy that is "created" is actually the creative energy of Infinite Intelligence, attracted and adding to the energy of the group. Anyone who has been a part of this kind of group knows the truth of this statement, and that it is a real phenomenon.

Attraction

We attract to ourselves the energy of our thoughts, for good or ill.

When it comes to energy, vibration and frequency, like attracts like. This can be said in many ways. We can refer to similar or harmonic vibration, or to being "in tune" with a certain frequency, on the same wavelength, or at the same energy level. However we choose to say it, we are attracted to things that we are "in sync" with; thoughts or ideas that are in harmony with our desires. It doesn't matter if those things are places, people, ideas or Infinite Intelligence; energy from Infinite Intelligence is attracted to the kind of energy we have within us. Seek and ye shall find, knock and it shall be opened.

Draw nigh to God, and he will draw nigh to you. – James 4:8

The Law of Attraction, although it is actually a secondary law to the Law of Vibration, is probably the most popular of the spiritual laws. It has gained a huge fan following from movies, sermons, lectures, books and short videos by the hundreds. Remember that it is part of the spiritual laws, and an important one, but not the only one. It could also be considered a part of the Law of Cause and Effect, described below. The spiritual laws work together to produce growth, understanding, realization of goals, and physical manifestation of ideas. Application of the spiritual laws can produce changes in our own state of energy and make changes in the flow of universal energy. However, focusing on just one of the laws by itself, like the Law of Attraction, will produce little growth. It will cause only a tiny increase in understanding and will almost certainly not get you to your goal. To attain a goal takes a concerted effort. That means all of the laws must be utilized in unison and harmony, like instruments and voices in a symphonic concert. All of the laws must also be used and applied properly, as well as other principles like persistence, faith, focus and gratitude, discussed later.

The Law of Attraction is similar to the physical law of attraction and repulsion, but has an important difference. Like the natural law dealing with electrical charge and magnetism, there are opposites: positive and negative or north and south. But the similarity ends there. In the spiritual Law of Attraction, things with the same nature are attracted to each other. Positive vibration or positive energy attracts more positive energy, which increases the positive vibration. Things with opposite natures repel each other.

So how does the Law of Attraction work? How is it possible for you to attract things to you that you want? It is because the Law of Attraction works in conjunction with the Law of Vibration. Vibrations of the same frequency are attracted to each another since they are "in tune" with each other, like the tuned guitar strings described above in the physical Law of Vibration.

In the spiritual sense, opposites repel each other, and like is attracted to like. We can see this in everyday life. There are commonly used terms that describe friends and good relationships: "We are on the same wavelength," or "We are in sync." We have friends that are like we are and have similar values because we are attracted to each other. Positive thoughts attract other positive thoughts or positive energy. Negative thoughts attract negative energy. Many of the phrases that are common in human language express this truth. "Birds of a feather flock together." "A person is known by the company he or she keeps." People who enjoy certain sports are attracted to others who enjoy the same sports. If you are a baseball fan, find another baseball fan and you have found a new friend, especially if the other person likes the same team you do!

The Law of Attraction can also be seen in the workplace. If three people with a positive, optimistic outlook toward their job and life in general work together, they enjoy their job and often will become good friends. The workplace has a light, easy vibe, the days are productive and fun, and as a result the business prospers. Throw a couple of other people into the same company with negative, complaining and resentful attitudes, and they will not "click" with the first three. But the two will certainly get along with each other! This new couple will commiserate and encourage each other to find things to be upset about. Together they can actually damage the working environment. Two opposing "camps" will be set up. The negative group will start to undermine anything positive that the positive group does. Friendships will be pulled apart by rumor and suspicion created by the negative employees, and the business will suffer as a result.

I'm sure many of you have seen this very thing happen in your workplace. The business will stop growing. An employee with a negative attitude is expensive. I was told once that if I looked at the employees where I work, there would be at least one person who has a negative attitude, and everyone knows who that person is. As the boss, if I were to tell that person that I would pay him or her their full salary on the condition that they never come to work, the business would make more money and run more smoothly. And it's true!

If you desire to attract God, Infinite Intelligence, through thoughts, intentions or prayer, God will respond. God will move closer to you if you desire to move closer to God. It is amazing to me that your desire alone can move the power of God toward you! How is this possible? By the Law of Attraction. This Law is absolutely true and does not change. It cannot be changed, just like you cannot get rid of the law of gravity. Your intense desire sends out a signal, a thought, a frequency of vibration, like a radio beacon. That signal is immediately received by Infinite Intelligence and causes a harmonic response in the universe. The response is the attraction of like to like, and the harmonic frequency of Infinite Intelligence moves toward you.

> *Hear ye me… The LORD is with you, while ye be with him; and if ye seek him, he will be found of you…* – 2 Chronicles 15:2

In the record that we have, Jesus spent more time on one aspect of the Law of Attraction than on almost any other topic dealing with attracting God's infinite energy to help us reach goals. He repeated over and over one of the basic premises of the Law of Attraction.

> *Ask, and it shall be given you; seek, and ye shall find; knock, and it shall be opened unto you: For every one that asketh receiveth; and he that seeketh findeth; and to him that knocketh it shall be opened.* – Matthew 7:7,8 Luke 11:9

This is probably the most well-known of the verses dealing with asking and receiving. Let's break down the parts here. Look at the sentence. There are three verbs here: ask, seek, and knock. This is important. What exactly is asking? It is expressing a desire, a longing, an outcome that you want to achieve, by taking action in the form of presenting a petition or request. Seeking, or actively looking, and knocking, making a noise at a door, are also actions stimulated by desire or need. Jesus repeated essentially the same thought three times in this one verse. He also made it very clear, between the lines, that desire alone is not enough. It must be followed by taking action, doing something to send the signal of desire out to Infinite Intelligence.

Strong desire followed by action produces results.

Several years ago I had a desire for a companion in my life. I thought about it and asked myself, "What would this person be like? What qualities of character am I seeking for my life companion?" So I sat down with my notebook to make a list, which I called "The Other List – the person I want as my life partner." I started to write mostly single adjectives that would describe to me the qualities of character of my ideal partner. The more I thought about it, the longer the list grew. And grew. I sat the notebook aside and came back the next day. The list grew longer. When it was finished, it had grown to sixty-two qualities of character! As I looked it over, I shook my head. Something inside me said, "Man, you just talked yourself out of a deal! There's no way that person exists," but another part of me said, "Let's see. Just wait." That page in my notebook was dated January 8. I closed the notebook and only looked at "The Other" list a couple times afterward. But the signal had been sent out.

Life went on and I was busy; working, raising my daughter, building a few surfboards for local surfers, and surfing when I could, until one day in August when a car drove into my driveway. Really! A car drove into my driveway and a woman whom I barely knew, another surfer, Sharen, got out and asked me if I would make her a new surfboard. I asked her what kind of board she currently had, and she told me she had three boards. I asked if I could see them.

It turned out she lived only two miles away. A few days later I met her outside her garage, where she showed me the boards. I looked at each one carefully then told her, "These are all good boards. Surf on them."

"But I don't like the way they work," she replied.

I told her, "Just use these. They are perfectly good. I won't make you a board. Sorry." And I left.

A few weeks later she was back in my driveway. A mutual friend had encouraged her to talk to me again. As we talked that day, standing in the driveway, a spark was ignited. Years later, I found that notebook and again read "The Other" list. Sixty-two qualities that perfectly described my wife, my life companion, my best friend. We still celebrate that August day in the driveway. Sharen now has three surfboards which I have made for her, and I carry the notebook with me in my man purse with "The Other" page still in it, just so I can look at it sometimes and smile. The Law of Attraction.

> *Hitherto have ye asked nothing in my name: ask, and ye shall receive, that your joy may be full.* – John 16:24

The Law of Attraction can also be used to shape your social environment. Everyone is attracted to people who think in the same way and hold similar values. If you have a negative outlook on life, you will attract to yourself a group of friends with negative outlooks on life because like attracts like. If at some point you desire to change your outlook and start to look on the positive side of life's experiences, you will have a difficult time in your old negative social group. You will not be on the same wavelength as they are. Conversations will be limited and uncomfortable because your friends will want to find things that aren't working, when you want to find things that are working. Eventually these friends will distance themselves from you because you are no longer in harmony. You do not share the same perspective about life.

At the same time, your new, positive outlook will begin to attract other people with a similar positive outlook, and a new group of positive friends will replace your old, negative group. In this new environment, you will discover even more things to be positive about!

The Law of Attraction can be used to shape your professional, financial and relationship worlds in the same way, leading to expansion, growing success and income, and more satisfying relationships.

You might find it hard to accept that God, Infinite Intelligence, would draw near to you just because you desire to draw near to God, but here is a most important fact. Remember that God is omnipresent; one hundred percent present in every part of the universe, equally, at every moment. And that includes within you. You have been created in the image of God, with the characteristics of God. Infinite intelligence, infinite energy, and infinite resources are available to you. All of this is within every cell of your body, filling the space occupied by your thoughts. "The kingdom of God is within you!" God is always within you, even when you don't recognize it or accept it. The energy of Infinite Intelligence is always flowing into you. God's creative nature is your creative nature. You have been created a creator. "We are all gods." So it really isn't too much to accept that God will draw near to us when we draw near to God. We don't really have to go anywhere, and neither does God.

But something is required. Here's an illustration:

Imagine you have been working outside in the heat of a scorching summer day. You are thirsty and go into the house to get a drink. Now imagine you are standing in your kitchen. Think of your sink. See it on the screen of your mind. There it is in front of you, metal or ceramic or granite. See the sink. Since you are thirsty, you reach up and open the door of the cabinet that has the glasses in it. Take out a glass. It is cool and smooth in your hand. Now reach out and turn on the faucet. Let it run for a second. Put the glass under the running water and hear the water running in. How good it sounds! The glass gets heavier as it fills up. You can hardly wait to quench your thirst. Hold the glass up to your lips and start drinking. Taste the water. Feel its cool, refreshing flow as your thirst is quenched.

Now think for a minute. Where did the water come from? The water was already there, in the pipes, inside the walls of your house, waiting. All you had to do to get the water flowing is turn the handle on a faucet. Drawing near to God and having God draw near to you, is really more like making the water flow. It is already in your house. It fills the pipes built inside the walls. To fulfill your desire to quench your thirst, it's just a matter of opening the faucet and letting the water flow. You take action, and the water flows into the glass. Does that make sense?

There are three very important things to remember in order to open the way for the Law of Attraction to really be effective in your life. I've called them steps, but they do not need to be in sequence. They just need to be applied to make the gears turn freely.

The first step: the power of asking in a positive way.

This first part of the Law of Attraction, the statement of desire, has an important application when you start setting personal goals. It is very important that when you visualize a goal, you begin to tell yourself what your goal is. Wording is vitally important. Remember that Infinite Intelligence does not recognize positive or negative conditions placed on a statement. It only responds to the subject of the sentence, the essential vibration. It does not hear words like "not," "don't," "won't" or "can't." So if I say, "I don't want to hit my thumb with the hammer again," the only part of the sentence recognized by the Infinite Intelligence is the "hit my thumb with the hammer", not the "I don't want." The response is to the main thought, not to the conditional word. If I word it this way, I get what I ask for, and I hit my thumb with the hammer! Your goal must be stated in positive terms if you want positive results. A better way to phrase this desire would be, "I am careful and hit the nail accurately." This makes a huge difference in your positive outlook, commitment, and in the results sent to you by Infinite Intelligence.

Take the statement "I'm not going to work with another person who is passive aggressive!" Guess what? The universe does not hear the "not" in the sentence, and I am doomed to work with another passive aggressive co-worker! Try to restate this in positive terms. What would you guess would be attracted if you say, "I don't want to be so poor or have so many bills that I can't pay them"? The more emotional you get about it and the stronger you affirm this kind of statement, the less money and more bills you will see, only because you have made a very successful negative expression of desire.

> *Finally, brethren, whatsoever things are true, whatsoever things are honest, whatsoever things are just, whatsoever things are pure, whatsoever things are lovely, whatsoever things are of good report; if there be any virtue, and if there be any praise, think on these things. – Philippians 4:8*

You know that you become what you think about. Affirmations are an excellent way to get yourself on track to becoming more than what you are right now: more spiritual, more prosperous, more giving, more understanding. When you are writing or saying affirmations concerning things in your life that you want to change or become, it is important that you focus on the things you want to achieve or attract into your life, not on what you don't want. If you focus on things you don't want, what happens is you get more of that thing which you don't want. Think about the person you want to be. Think about the life you want to live.

The second step: I AM

Whenever you make an affirmation, it should be stated in the present tense, not with the weak and vague "I will" or "I want to" introductions. Give your affirmations power by stating them in present tense, believing they have already happened. "I am fit and strong." "I work with a supportive person." Phrase the sentence as a positive statement, in the present tense, so when the thought energy goes out there is no mistaking your intention. I am happy and grateful…

This is actually a good practice to start in every part of your life. Starting today, word every statement in a positive way. It's not about what you don't want, it's all about what you are, and being the person (in the present tense: I am…) you want to be. Once positive statements become a habit, you will notice a change in the way you view the world. This is because you will have eliminated from your own subconscious mind the belief that the world is a place filled with things you don't want, or things that you may receive someday in the future, if nothing interferes. You will start to see yourself as the person you ARE. Remember, you are a part of Infinite Intelligence; you are a creator; you are your future!

The third step: everyone wins!

Finally, remember the Golden Rule. It is important that your intention in asking is not just for yourself. Think of "give and it shall be given" and the Golden Rule: Do unto others as you would have others do unto you.

Many people love money and use people. That is backwards, and does not lead to true prosperity. Use money, but love people.

Belief

Jesus understood very well the Law of Attraction. He focused on this Law, perhaps more than any other principle. He wanted people to understand it, to believe that we can ask for anything, to believe that God moves in response to our request, makes it so, and brings it into being. We are created as creators. One of the ways to open the valve, to allow the energy of Infinite Intelligence to flow toward us, is belief.

> *Jesus said unto him, If thou canst believe, all things are possible to him that believeth.* – Mark 9:23

There is no limit put on this promise. No restrictions at all. The only condition is that you believe that Infinite Intelligence has the ability to do that which you ask, and responds to your request. Many people simply will not accept this promise for what it is: a promise without condition other than belief that it will be so. People will say, "Jesus didn't mean this literally. He was only speaking in the abstract, about receiving spiritual growth." This is not true. Jesus made it unquestionably clear, over and over.

> *Believest thou not that I am in the Father, and the Father in me? The words that I speak unto you I speak not of myself: but the Father that dwelleth in me, he doeth the works. Believe me that I am in the Father, and the Father in me: or else believe me for the very works' sake. Verily, verily, I say unto you, He that believeth on me, the works that I do shall he do also; and greater works than these shall he do...* – John 14:10-12

It is difficult to imagine that the last sentence of this quotation is true. "Greater works than these shall he do..." But Jesus was even more specific about the power of the Law of Attraction to accomplish the seemingly impossible:

> *Verily I say unto you, If ye have faith, and doubt not, ye shall not only do this which is done to the fig tree, but also if ye shall say unto this mountain, Be thou removed, and be thou cast into the sea; it shall be done.* – Matthew 21:21

He even used examples from everyday family life, referring to the love of a parent toward a child.

> *If ye then... know how to give good gifts unto your children, how much more shall your Father which is in heaven give good things to them that ask him?* – Matthew 7:11

There is also a reference to people who meet together to achieve a common goal. It is absolutely clear that there is no limit to what we can accomplish by focusing our thoughts toward achieving a worthy goal. It is also clear that the promise is not limited to spiritual topics because it is agreed on earth as touching any thing.

Again I say unto you, That if two of you shall agree on earth as touching any thing that they shall ask, it shall be done for them of my Father which is in heaven. – Matthew 18:19

Jesus also gives specific examples of things that may be asked which seem to be impossible:

And the Lord said, If ye had faith as a grain of mustard seed, ye might say unto this sycamine tree, Be thou plucked up by the root, and be thou planted in the sea; and it should obey you. – Luke 17:6

This concept was not only hard for the common people in Jesus' day to comprehend and accept, it was also difficult for the Disciples. To really emphasize the importance and power of the Law of Attraction, Jesus felt it was necessary to repeat this same concept over and over, even in the same lesson that he was teaching. In the book of John, Jesus repeated the same thing, "ask and ye shall receive," seven times in three consecutive chapters, each time wording the promise a little differently. As a teacher, I know this technique. If the students don't quite get it when it's said one way, try to word it a little differently. Eventually the light will go on.

Why do ye not understand my speech? – John 8:43

At one point, Jesus was answering questions posed by His disciples. To make his point as clearly as possible, that whatever we ask will be given to us by Infinite Intelligence, He repeated this idea several times in three consecutive chapters.

And whatsoever ye shall ask in my name, that will I do, that the Father may be glorified in the Son. – John 14:13

If ye shall ask any thing in my name, I will do it. – John 14:14

> *If ye abide in me, and my words abide in you, ye shall ask what ye will, and it shall be done unto you.* – John 15:7

> *…that whatsoever ye shall ask of the Father in my name, he may give it you.* – John 15:16

> *Hitherto have ye asked nothing in my name: ask, and ye shall receive, that your joy may be full.* – John 16:24

Jesus wanted us to understand that asking and receiving from God, Infinite Intelligence, is a Spiritual Law. Ask in a positive way, believe that God has heard and given what you ask, make your request for the benefit of yourself and others, then let God fulfill the Law. Ask with the assurance that you have the Law on your side, and it will come to pass.

> *But let him ask in faith, nothing wavering. For he that wavereth is like a wave of the sea driven with the wind and tossed.*
> – James 1:6

The Apostle John even heard in his Revelation the voice of Jesus speaking about this Law of Attraction, but in this case, it was Jesus doing the knocking, attracted to each of us. When you "hear… and open the door" that is your response, like attracted to like, that allows Jesus, Infinite Intelligence, to come in and share energy from the infinite reserve.

> *Behold, I stand at the door, and knock: if any man hear my voice, and open the door, I will come in to him, and will sup with him, and he with me.* – Revelation 3:20

Cause and Effect

The spiritual Law of Cause and Effect, called by Ralph Waldo Emerson the "Law of Laws," is the spiritual analog of the physical Law of Action and Reaction. The Law of Cause and Effect comprises several specific types of cause and effect, which are often presented as laws in themselves. I have no disagreement with that. It's a little like the world of bird biologists. There are splitters and lumpers. Some ornithologists want to divide birds into different species and subspecies based on various physical, geographic or behavioral traits. Others want to group them into larger groups based on similarities and reproductive success. I guess I am a bit of a lumper. I have taken the liberty to put the laws with similarities under one umbrella.

The separate aspects of the Law of Cause and Effect are: Action and Reaction, Sowing and Reaping, Compensation, and Reciprocity (or Karma). Each of these will be covered separately, but first I'll tell a brief story that introduces some of these aspects.

As a young adult in the 1970s, I was intent on living off the land. My family had a large garden, and I decided that I was going to make bread, literally from scratch. So I bought some wheat and planted it in one area of the garden. Since we had a cow and chickens, the soil was well fertilized. The wheat sprouted and grew through the summer, like tall grass. In late August it was golden and beautiful, with heads full of wheat grains nodding down from the tips. I carefully cut it with my vintage wooden scythe. I was enthusiastic about mowing the wheat, but after a few minutes realized that I was grateful to have only planted a small patch. Cutting by hand is exhausting! I stripped the wheat from the straw, separated the grains from the chaff, and spread the grains of wheat out to dry.

Even though the individual grains had multiplied several times, there were only enough of them to fill a couple cookie sheets. The wheat spent all day in the sun drying. In the kitchen, I had set up a cast iron hand grinder with a long handle. The grain was poured into a small, metal cup at the top of the grinder. It filtered down between two grinding wheels that crushed the wheat into smaller and smaller pieces with each pass. It took four passes to get something that coarsely resembled flour. There was just enough flour to make one loaf of bread.

The rest of the process was a normal bread recipe with yeast, salt and water. Mix, rise, punch down, rise again. The freshly ground, coarse flour didn't behave like flour from the market. It rose, but just enough to make a dense loaf. Into the oven it went. When it was done, it looked more like a piece of firewood than a loaf of bread, but I was not disappointed. That loaf of bread was hearty and delicious, and enjoyed by the whole family! I had set my mind to make bread, and did it! It only took three months from start to finish. That bread was the first and last bread I made from seed.

This is a story about cause and effect, in many different ways. Of course, there is the overall intention of making the bread, the cause, and the finished loaf, the effect. The wheat also took sowing and reaping, and there were cycles of action and reaction in the cutting, grinding and baking of the bread.

But the story contains a deeper lesson. Think of yourself as the wheat. In life, most changes take time. I had a neighbor whose son went out to the garden and started "planting" Cheerios. He was planning to grow doughnuts! A finished loaf of bread doesn't just grow out of the ground. Changes have to happen first. The wheat seeds must be planted. They absorb light, attract water and nutrients from the soil using chemotaxis, grow and multiply, all according to natural laws, and in an appropriate time. The effect is abundance. Fresh wheat can't be made directly into bread, it has to be crushed again and again then mixed with yeast to make it expand, and put into the oven to make the finished loaf.

Sometimes you may feel like your growth isn't as fast or as abundant as you would like it to be. Remember, everything takes its own time. Life may seem at times to run you through the grinder. And then there's the oven! These times in life change and add character and flavor to our life. We've all been through it, but when the process is finished, we come out changed, nutritious and savory, something that can be shared with others.

Action and Reaction

The dance of Infinite Intelligence has many facets. If you think of partners in a ballroom dance, you may be able to visualize some aspects of the Law of Action and Reaction. One partner advances, the other retreats. One spins, the other is there to support. Leaping and catching are choreographed and well-practiced in order to be executed flawlessly; a push and a pull, followed by attraction and more attraction. These are parts that create the beauty of dance and correlate well to the dance of life.

Every action we take has a reaction. Every time. Like in the physical world, the reaction is always equal and opposite. For every effect there is always a cause. Growth is always the result of planting and nurturing the young plants. If we decide our goal is to become more intuitive in our dealings with other people and apply ourselves to learning about how to increase intuition, the effect will be an increase in our intuitive "radar" and we will find that we become more accurate in reading the backstory of why people act the way they do, the strengths of their personalities, or the emotional background of how they present themselves.

Knowledge is an effect, caused, in one way, by studying. Knowledge is the accumulation of information. If you want to be an expert in any subject, one thing you must do is study, study, study. By reading about your subject, you reap the benefit of other people's work. You learn what they know. As Newton would have said, you stand on the shoulders of giants. If you are persistent in studying, you will eventually have gained enough information to be an expert in your subject. Study and dedication will have produced their effect.

If we send out positive energy, positive energy will return to us. Resistance restricts expansion. Thoughts of prosperity result in prosperity. Asking is necessary if receiving is to be gained. If we want to receive, we first need to give.

Sowing and Reaping

There are many verses in the Bible which relate to agriculture. This was a topic well known to the people of Jesus' day. Theirs was an agrarian civilization, and their lives depended on knowledge and successful application of the principles of growth, how to achieve abundant reproduction, and harvesting when the fields were ripe. The percentage of people engaged in agriculture today is much lower than it was two thousand years ago, but our civilization still depends on the same laws. And, "as above, so below," the parables of sowing and reaping are still true today.

> *Be not deceived; God is not mocked: for whatsoever a man soweth, that shall he also reap.* – Galatians 6:7

This verse is often shortened to "as you sow, so shall you reap." It is interesting to think of the way this concept is usually applied in life. From our early years we are often conditioned by our genetics and environment to see things in a negative light, unless we were blessed to have parents who understood the spiritual laws. Because of this, what we might read into the above verse is a warning, to be careful and don't do the wrong thing or hang out with the wrong people. This advice is repeated by parents and may be intended to be helpful. Even Paul spends some time writing about negative choices, but he does end by saying, "let us do good unto all." While the negative is true, so is the positive. In agricultural terms we follow the law. We sow good seed in abundance, sow into soil which is rich and well prepared to receive seed, tend to the weeds diligently, and water and fertilize at the proper time. This maximizes the positive outcome: reap in abundance and enjoy a bountiful harvest.

It is important that you "be not deceived," and think that because positive thoughts and actions sometimes take time to manifest the good we desire, that the Law of Sowing and Reaping is incorrect. That is not true. When you focus your creative mind on positive thoughts and take action, positive changes in your life will be produced and you will move closer to your desired goal. It must be this way because it is a Spiritual Law.

Think of growing green beans. The bean seeds are planted sometime in May. Poles and twine are added in early June. The beans grow, wind around the poles and twine, and blossom in midsummer, but it's not until the middle or end of July that you can expect to start picking green beans for the table. Farming is not fast food! You can't plant potatoes and expect French fries by the time you get back to the house. The time it takes to see results is part of the Laws of Rhythm and Gender, which cover the gestation of life. Be patient.

> *But this I say, He which soweth sparingly shall reap also sparingly; and he which soweth bountifully shall reap also bountifully. – 2 Corinthians 9:6*

Focus on thoughts of bounty: abundance, prosperity, gratitude, giving back. These are the kinds of positive thoughts you need to sow in the fertile soil of your own subconscious mind in order to reap the fruit of a prosperous, abundant life.

> *And God said, Let the earth bring forth grass, the herb yielding seed, and the fruit tree yielding fruit after his kind, whose seed is in itself, upon the earth: and it was so. And the earth brought forth grass, and herb yielding seed after his kind, and the tree yielding fruit, whose seed was in itself, after his kind: and God saw that it was good. – Genesis 1:11-12*

From the opening page of Genesis, the Law of Sowing and Reaping was explained. It is part of the wonder of life. Every living thing produces seeds which grow into the next generation, and the next generation has characteristics similar to the parents. Peach trees produce peaches. Peach pits from the peaches grow into new peach trees, and the cycle perpetuates itself.

> *Ye shall know them by their fruits. Do men gather grapes of thorns, or figs of thistles? Even so every good tree bringeth forth good fruit… – Matthew 7:16-17*

A gardener would be shocked to find tomatoes growing where corn had been planted. In fact, it would be so against everything the gardener knew that she or he would suspect that someone planted tomato seeds, and crows ate all the corn! If I plant beans, I expect bean plants. And not just any bean plants. Lima beans do not grow from pinto beans. It goes against the Law of Sowing and Reaping.

Jesus described the concepts of sowing and reaping, regeneration and abundance in what is called the Parable of the Sower:

> *A sower went out to sow his seed: and as he sowed, some fell by the way side; and it was trodden down, and the fowls of the air devoured it. And some fell upon a rock; and as soon as it was sprung up, it withered away, because it lacked moisture. And*

> *some fell among thorns; and the thorns sprang up with it, and choked it. And other fell on good ground, and sprang up, and bare fruit an hundredfold. And when he had said these things, he cried, He that hath ears to hear, let him hear.* – Luke 8:5-8, Matthew 13:3-9, Mark 4:1-9

Jesus made the Law of Sowing and Reaping clear. Every living thing produces fruit. The fruit contains the seeds of life which reproduce offspring similar to the parent.

In the spiritual application of the Law of Sowing and Reaping, the same principle is true. Good thoughts acted upon with good intention produce good results, the offspring of the original thoughts. Thoughts of prosperity will produce prosperity. Thoughts of abundance will produce abundance, but only if the other conditions are met. There must be intention and action. Seeds must be planted in fertile soil, and they must be watered and cared for. If the seed is from a fruit tree, the tree may need to be pruned seasonally. Attention must be given, and work must be done or the seed will not successfully mature.

A wise man once told me, "Anyone can count the number of seeds in an apple. But no one can count the number of apples in a seed." I have heard statements which inspire me to be better than I am, change the way I live, and grow. These statements, these seeds of inspiration, are living things, planted in my heart. They sprout and grow, like the seeds of all living things. Nurtured, watered and fed, they produce fruit and more seeds. I am grateful for the seeds that have been planted in me, and for the next generation of seeds they have produced.

Compensation

This special area of the Law of Cause and Effect is sometimes called the Law of Reciprocity: when two parties exchange something which gives them mutual benefit. This happens in most jobs. The employer/employee relationship is a good example of this area of Cause and Effect because the tasks the employee performs comprise the Cause, and Compensation or Salary is the Effect. An employee exchanges a task, skill or intellectual expertise for some agreed-upon payment, usually in terms of money.

Jesus said:

> ...*the labourer is worthy of his hire.* – Matthew 10:7

This is the Law of Cause and Effect as it relates to achieving Abundance and Wealth. A person receives exactly the value of what he or she renders in terms of service. If the service rendered is exceptional, the compensation should be equally exceptional.

There are three rules of compensation that are always in effect. Your value in your work is in direct proportion to:

1. The need for what you do.
2. Your ability to do it.
3. The degree of difficulty there is in replacing you.

When you are thinking of these three aspects of the Law of Compensation, you should focus most of your energy on your ability to do it. Choose a line of work that you love and that is needed. Then, if you think like the owner of a company and devote your time in the most focused, efficient and productive way you can, you really don't have to concern yourself about being replaced because you will be irreplaceable. The laborer is worthy of her or his hire.

The Law of Compensation was described well in another of Jesus' best known parables, called the Parable of the Talents. First, a few prefatory comments:

When we are babies, we can really do nothing for ourselves. We are totally dependent upon the care of our parents, but as we grow physically, we also grow in our ability to take care of ourselves. We learn how to walk, run, communicate, and eventually follow directions. That happens sooner for some than for others, as many parents know. We learn skills according to our abilities. If we have a natural knack in a particular area, it is called a gift or a talent. All of you probably know a talented artist, singer or writer. Some people have a talent in handling money, talking with people or knowing how to heal a person in one way or another. Let's look for a moment at the word talent, with some historical perspective.

It is interesting to me that one of the ancient units of currency in the Mediterranean region was called a talent. This "talent" is actually a measure of weight. Although the exact equivalent weight in modern measurement is not clear from historic records (there were Hebrew, Roman and Greek talents), it is believed to be slightly more than sixty pounds (US). The Roman talent was the weight of one cubic foot of water, so a talent of silver in today's money would be worth about $17,000, and a talent of gold would be worth about $1.3 million. In the parable of the talents, let's assume the talent mentioned is a talent of silver. Whichever it was when Jesus told the Parable of the Talents, the amount of money entrusted to the servants was significant. The knack or gift that we call a "talent" today is also something of very great value, not to be taken for granted!

The Parable of the Talents

For *the kingdom of heaven* is as a man travelling into a far country, who called his own servants, and delivered unto them his goods. And unto one he gave five talents, to another two, and to another one; to every man according to his several ability; and straightway took his journey. Then he that had received the five talents went and traded with the same, and made them other five talents. And likewise he that had received two, he also gained other two. But he that had received one went and digged in the earth, and hid his lord's money.

After a long time the lord of those servants cometh, and reckoneth with them. And so he that had received five talents came and brought other five talents, saying, Lord, thou delivered unto me five talents: behold, I have gained beside them five talents more. His lord said unto him, Well done, thou good and faithful servant: thou hast been faithful over a few things, I will make thee ruler over many things: enter thou into the joy of thy lord.

He also that had received two talents came and said, Lord, thou delivered unto me two talents: behold, I have gained two other talents beside them. His lord said unto him, Well done, good and faithful servant; thou hast been faithful over a few things, I will make thee ruler over many things: enter thou into the joy of thy lord.

> Then he which had received the one talent came and said, Lord, I knew thee that thou art an hard man, reaping where thou hast not sown, and gathering where thou hast not strawed: And I was afraid, and went and hid thy talent in the earth: lo, there thou hast that is thine.
>
> His lord answered and said unto him, Thou wicked and slothful servant, thou knewest that I reap where I sowed not, and gather where I have not strawed: Thou ought therefore to have put my money to the exchangers, and then at my coming I should have received mine own with usury [interest]. Take therefore the talent from him, and give it unto him which hath ten talents.
>
> For unto every one that hath shall be given, and he shall have abundance. – Matthew 25:14-29, Luke 19:11-26

We are all talented and gifted. It's what we do with the talent and the gift that sets us apart.

It is clear from the parable that we are expected to do something with our talents, the natural gifts that have been given to us. God wants us, even encourages us to expand, grow and increase the talents we have been given, to make the world a better place.

> *And God blessed them, and God said unto them, Be fruitful, and multiply… – Genesis 1:28*

We each have within us great untapped reservoirs of talent, but often we either do not recognize our gifts or we are held back from developing them by fear and doubt. We let our imaginations conjure up criticism, feelings of unworthiness or inability, or we cover up our fear with excuses like, "I'm too busy," "My (family, coworkers, students, boss) need me to be doing other things." Remember that doubt and fear are only imaginary. They are not real. The only thing that can hold you back are your own thoughts. The bottom line is, you have a talent. Probably several, if you think about it. In order to be the person that you are meant to be, you need to nourish that talent, strengthen it, let it flourish and grow, and see what other talents you have that you haven't even thought of. Talent is an open door to a path of fulfillment, prosperity and an abundant life. Take advantage of it!

Reciprocity

It is often said, "What goes around, comes around."

There is another aspect to this part of the Law of Cause and Effect called Reciprocity. This idea is common to many faiths. In the Hindu faith it is called karma. If the energy which I send out to the world is positive, I will gain positive energy in my life. If I give out negative energy, I will receive negative energy in return. It may not happen right away, but it will happen. This is in direct correlation with the Law of Attraction. In rural American vernacular, receiving negative energy back is called "gettin' your comeuppance." If I act from a place of positive energy, the good that I do will be returned to me.

This is the basis of what is often called the "Golden Rule":

> *Therefore all things whatsoever ye would that men should do to you, do ye even so to them: for this is the law and the prophets.* – Matthew 7:12

> *And as ye would that men should do to you, do ye also to them likewise.* – Luke 6:31

This part of the Law is sometimes called the Law of Giving and Receiving. To receive, you must first have the spirit of giving. In other words:

> *Give, and it shall be given unto you... For with the same measure that ye mete withal it shall be measured to you again.* – Luke 6:38

Giving and Receiving can work both ways since the Law of Attraction says what energy we send out will attract the same type of energy back to us. Remember this fact. How you feel or act toward others will come back to you, and you want that energy to be positive! This was as true in the days of Solomon or Jesus as it is today.

> *Then said Jesus unto him, Put up again thy sword into his place: for all they that take the sword shall perish with the sword.* – Matthew 26:52

Judge not, and ye shall not be judged: condemn not, and ye shall not be condemned. – Luke 6:37

What goes around, comes around.

Jesus was making an important point. When we send a thought out into the universe, the intention of that thought, the energy or frequency or vibration of the thought energy, returns to us. Remember, like attracts like. Be careful what thoughts you have toward those that are your professional associates, friends, family, and even yourself. Like attracts like.

Modern media encourages the production of negative thoughts, and is successful in drawing them out of an audience that has no idea how powerful those thoughts are. It's no wonder that negativity continues to grow in the world!

In a more positive sense,

> *...forgive, and ye shall be forgiven... Give, and it shall be given unto you; good measure, pressed down, and shaken together, and running over, shall men give into your bosom...*
> – Luke 6:37-38

The message is clear. If you desire abundance, give. If you need forgiveness, forgive others and yourself. The giving or forgiving needs to be done in a spirit of trust that what you need will come to you as a result of your first giving or forgiving.

Any positive thought which goes out from your mind will return positive energy back to you. Conversely, negative energy going out produces negative energy coming back. Actions which I take toward others will return to me in a similar way and quality.

Jesus was referring to the Law of Reciprocity and the Law of Attraction when He said:

> *Blessed are they which do hunger and thirst after righteousness: for they shall be filled.* – Matthew 5:6

> *Blessed are the merciful: for they shall obtain mercy.*
> – Matthew 5:7

Polarity and Relativity

Polarity

A World of Opposites

Hot and cold. Up and down. Tiny and huge. Light and Dark. The universe has a multitude of qualities which are found in pairs on a continuum, a scale like a spectrum that has extremes at both ends, which we call opposites. The opposite ends are often called polar opposites, like the north and south poles of the earth or the poles of a magnet, and thus the name polarity. We use these scales to compare things, to put them in some kind of order, and to define a little more clearly the world around us.

On the other hand, there are some qualities which do not have exact opposites. What is the opposite of brown? How about the opposite of tree or rock or spoon? We scratch our heads to come up with an opposite for some things because there is no exact opposite. But for many, many qualities there is a continuous scale on which that quality is found. It is this scale or continuum upon which we will focus our attention.

There are many ways to describe the world we live in. One way is to look at how many opposites there are. There is no up without a down, no day without night. In order to know hot, we compare it to cold. The emotion of love is the opposite of fear and cannot dwell in the same place. Good and evil have existed forever. Freedom and bondage go back for ages and tell the story of the human experience. Inside and outside, front and back, positive and negative, near and far, attraction and repulsion, male and female, yin and yang, life and death. The list is very long!

Opposites also help to give us perspective. By having two opposite qualities, we have a way of defining each one. We establish points of reference and varying shades of difference between the opposite or polar extremes. For example, in order to define size, we need some reference of large and small. Often we use our own bodies as the "midpoint." If an object takes up less space than we do, like a penny, we say that object is small. By comparison with a human, an elephant is large. A mountain may be huge compared to a person, but it is small compared to a continent.

We can't imagine "there" without understanding what "here" means. Acceptance and rejection are defined by perspective, along with hundreds of other qualities to which we give meaning by comparing them with other similar things along the same continuum. In *Hamlet*, Shakespeare said, "There is nothing either good or bad, but thinking makes it so." He spoke wise words about perspective.

It has been said, "When you change your view of the world, the world changes." This is another way of saying that perspective gives us a new way of evaluating the qualities of the world around us.

I was driving the family home along the freeway just after dark. It was one of those beautiful, autumn evenings, and a full moon was rising over the mountains to the east. Our daughter was in the back seat, quietly staring out the window. She was watching the moon intently. Suddenly she asked, "Daddy, why does the moon keep moving so fast through the trees?"

I told her, "It's called perspective, sweetie."

"Oh," she answered, and kept staring at the moon.

I went on. "When we drive fast, the trees are close so they look like they are going fast too. The moon is very far away, so it looks like it's not moving."

"'Spective," she said to herself, thinking.

Perspective is sometimes described as a point of view. It is also a physical phenomenon which has spiritual applications. It is perspective that allows us and all other animals that are hunters to accurately estimate distance. Animals which are lower on the food chain, like rabbits and chickens, have eyes on the sides of their heads and cannot see forward in the same way we can. We have both eyes facing forward, and each eye sees what is directly in front of us at a slightly different angle. We actually see two slightly different images. You can prove this to yourself by holding one thumb up in front of you and closing one eye. Stare at the background behind your thumb then switch eyes. When you do this, your thumb appears to make a sudden jump to one side! This is because of the change in perspective between your eyes. Now keep the background in focus and open both eyes. You can see two thumbs. By changing your focus and bringing the images together, you can judge how far away something is.

Spiritual perspective enables you to judge things too, but instead of how far away something is, you can judge values like honesty, whether an activity is the "right thing to do," or the importance of something that you feel is "close to you" by seeing it against the larger background of life.

In life, and in a spiritual sense, we can appreciate an open door when we have experienced a closed door. We understand the value of what we have in life if we have gone through the profound sense of loss when a person or pet we have loved passes away. Perspective that we get from opposite qualities gives us the ability to measure, compare and evaluate many of the qualities and experiences of life.

The juxtaposition of opposites is one of the elements of comedy. One classic comic premise which uses the humor of opposites is the messy person who lives with a neat freak. Opposites can create comedy because we can all relate to it. I know couples who are happily married, but the wife follows the husband around the house, constantly picking up his messes, and the husband is frustrated because he can never find where he "left" his keys or shoes.

Opposite qualities are good things, especially when we think of our place in the world and creating goals for our lives. When we want to improve ourselves, our desire is to change. We want to move in our life from where we are to where we want to be. We want to grow in understanding, wisdom and prosperity. We might want to become strong and flexible or to know more about how to access the internet. In order to accomplish higher goals for ourselves in life, we first need to define what we are now, what we want to have or become, and set our minds to acquire that. If we want to move from "here" to "there" we need to first define where "here" is, then we need to define where "there" is. Our goal, perhaps, is the ideal person we want to emulate, or the vision of success or prosperity for which we long. By defining that we want to become a better person, we can begin to move away from what we don't want, the opposite of what we want. Definition allows us to move toward the goal and avoid distractions. Perspective in the nontangible sense allows us to judge the distance between "here" and "there."

Here is another example of the importance of perspective. I was sitting at a round table in a large seminar, waiting for the seminar to resume after a break. As I talked to the person next to me, people were taking their seats. The person I was talking to shifted to make room for the person next to him, and as he shifted, I saw a flash of bright pink. Three tables over there was a woman who had been sitting in her seat wearing a fluorescent pink sweater, who had been completely hidden behind my friend. She was in my direct line of sight, but totally invisible behind my friend's body. I was suddenly made aware that I needed to be more conscious of the power of perspective, not only to give me a different point of view, but also to bring to my awareness something that was hidden in my direct line of vision because I was focused on something else very close at hand.

The Law of Polarity is as true in the physical world as in the nonphysical world, the world of thought, idea and emotion. Opposite qualities like Love and Fear, Apathy and Enthusiasm, Attraction and Repulsion, are not as easy to define, but every person has an intuitive understanding of them and the continuum upon which they are found. One person might say the opposite of love is fear, while another might say the opposite is hatred. Actually, fear is in fact the polar opposite of love. That is why it is said, "Perfect love casteth out fear." Still, the spiritual world has just as many opposites as the natural world.

When you set a goal for yourself, you may find the Law of Polarity becomes very real. Say you want to release the habit of smoking and you set that as a goal. You may find that within hours you are offered cigarettes from all kinds of people. This challenge is Infinite Intelligence showing you the opposite of Not Smoking. It is not "temptation" as some may call it. It is just the Law of Polarity in effect, and is powerful evidence that your goal of Not Smoking is taking you in the right direction because you have the opposite of Not Smoking thrown right in front of you for comparison.

Relativity

You can rest easy here. This is not the Relativity of Einstein that deals with strange changes at very high speeds or in the presence of gravitational fields. This Relativity is part of the Law of Polarity and deals with evaluating our life relative to other things in life.

Everyone receives a series of challenges in life. Whether they are called challenges, obstacles, situations or problems, they come into our lives to help us grow. Obstacles are not intended to beat us down or victimize us, but to strengthen us, teach us, and allow us to gain perspective.

In the days when I kept chickens, I had one young hen for whom all life was an obstacle. She had difficulty finding her way in and out of the hen house, and often even in finding her way out of the chicken run. Every morning I would open the gate to the chicken run to let the chickens wander around the pasture and even down to the creek to hunt for bugs. On several occasions, after all the other chickens were out rooting around in the grass and turning over leaves and sticks, this wayward hen was by herself inside the chicken run, poking her head through the chicken wire over and over. She would poke through, try to pick at some grass, move a few inches and poke through in another spot. She was intent on getting to the other side of the fence, but failed to see that the gate was propped wide open not twenty feet from where she was struggling.

Life was a challenge for her! She could see no way around that obstacle, the fence, that all the other hens had navigated with ease. Relative to all the other chickens, her life was hard. Eventually she discovered that if she copied exactly what the successful chickens did, she could walk right out into the pasture just like they did. At that point, I'm sure all of her chicken frustration vanished. An obstacle had been overcome. For weeks, that hen's life had been miserable relative to the other chickens.

During times of challenge, it is important to recognize that what appear to be obstacles in our path are really opportunities to find solutions, possibilities to become stronger, widen our perspective, and expand the horizon of our vision. By finding solutions, we grow in confidence and understanding. Every obstacle is an opportunity to learn, and by learning, by being successful, we can grow in our understanding and gratitude.

Napoleon Hill, one of the great teachers of how to achieve success in life said, "Every failure brings with it the seed of an equivalent success." Failure teaches us how to succeed.

Rhythm

In all of the movement in the universe, there are two constants: change and rhythm.

The Old Testament book of Ecclesiastes, attributed to David's son, King Solomon, contains a beautiful poetic description of the cycles of opposites in life:

> To every *thing there is* a season, and a time to every purpose under the heaven:
>
> A time to be born, and a time to die; a time to plant, and a time to pluck up *that which is* planted;
>
> A time to kill, and a time to heal; a time to break down, and a time to build up;
>
> A time to weep, and a time to laugh; a time to mourn, and a time to dance;
>
> A time to cast away stones, and a time to gather stones together; a time to embrace, and a time to refrain from embracing;
>
> A time to get, and a time to lose; a time to keep, and a time to cast away;
>
> A time to rend, and a time to sew; a time to keep silence, and a time to speak;
>
> A time to love, and a time to hate; a time of war, and a time of peace.
>
> – Ecclesiastes 3:1-6

Cycles and rhythms are an integral part of both the natural world and the spiritual world.

Day unto day uttereth speech, and night unto night sheweth knowledge. – Psalm 19:2

The natural world has untold thousands of different rhythms. Some are relatively slow, like the passing of a year, summer solstice to summer solstice, as the earth orbits around the sun. About every four weeks the moon circles the earth and goes through its cycles, called "phases". Day follows night, sunrise to sunset and back to sunrise, as the earth spins on its axis.

Rhythms in nature are produced by cyclic motion, which are exactly the same as vibrations. Everything in the universe is in a state of constant motion, and that motion is in rhythmic curved paths. On the surface of the ocean, waves pass every few seconds. Although the wave form appears to move in a linear way, the water particles that make up the wave are actually moving in circles, larger at the surface and progressively smaller as the water gets deeper. There are also examples of other cyclic movement: ellipses, like the path of planets and moons; figure eights, like the change in length of daylight as the seasons change (called the analemma); sine waves, like the vibration of a piano string; or the daily rise and fall of tides. This cyclic motion permeates everything in the universe and is present in everything from subatomic particles to galaxies.

Some rhythms are relatively fast, like the vibrations of sound waves. Audible sounds, the sounds we can hear in the human range, vibrate in the hundreds of cycles per second. Some of these frequencies are known to stimulate healing or creative thought. Light waves, heat waves and radio waves vibrate in the frequency of millions of cycles per second. Absolutely everything is moving in cyclic rhythm. Atoms vibrate and electrons spin. The number of different rhythms in nature is unimaginably large, and the time scale that envelopes the slowest to the fastest rhythms is just as enormous, from millionths of a second to hundreds of thousands of years.

Through all of these rhythms, energy is transformed or transmutated. Energy can move from one place to another, like the energy transferred by light or sound waves. Heat energy in the sun is transformed into light, which travels millions of miles to strike a person basking on a summer beach. Some of the energy is converted back into heat, and some is converted into chemical changes in the person's skin cells, which result in a suntan or sunburn.

Earlier we discussed some of the qualities of vibration and rhythm. The rate of vibration is called the frequency. The power of the vibration is the amplitude. Tiny water waves are of low amplitude. Huge crashing storm waves are high amplitude. In the case of sound waves, higher frequency means higher tone or pitch. Higher amplitude means louder sound. For light, frequency determines color, and amplitude refers to the brightness. All of these definitions related to vibrations are not things you need to memorize because they do not change your ability to appreciate the beauty of a sunset or the majesty of a stormy day at the ocean. In your heart you understand harmony of vibrations, and something within you resonates with what is called beauty, whether it is music, color, or inspiration of thoughts. But they are useful when we talk about vibrations and waves.

In the spiritual sense, the idea of rhythm can also be used to describe the frequency of a person's vibration. The quality of a person's vibration is shown by feeling or emotion. What we call "feeling" is the conscious awareness of our own vibration. Everyone has shifts of mood or feeling from time to time. These correspond to shifts in vibration, from positive to negative or from high frequency to low frequency. In the spiritual sense, low frequencies correspond to the "negative" vibrations: fear, apathy, antagonism, tension. High frequencies are the "positive" vibrations: love, gratitude, enthusiasm, serenity. Low amplitude may be the vibration of just one person formulating a goal or creating a new idea. High amplitude would exist in the enthusiastic brainstorming of a mastermind group, where the harmonic vibrations of many individuals are in sync and build upon one another to become very powerful.

Life has a myriad of cycles. One generation passes to a new generation. Temporary failure is followed by success. Problems in life are followed by solutions. Joy comes after a time of darkness. The cycle of birth, growth and birth again is endlessly repeated, and the great cycle of life continues. In all these cycles, energy is moving. A low point in a cycle is only a part of the cycle. Day follows night. The full moon always comes two weeks after the new.

I worked logging for a while on the Olympic peninsula in Washington State with a wise man from the mountains of West Virginia. We were taking a lunch break on a pleasant April day after weeks of dark, cold, winter weather. He said, "I like this kind of spring day. I can look forward to two summers ahead, with only one winter in between."

If you ever feel like you are at a low point, when the days seem short and cold, and the nights seem long, remember the Law of Rhythm. Energy is always moving and changing form, and in the natural cycle there is a rise and fall, like the tides. It is important in the "winter" of life that you remember to keep moving. The cyclic rhythm will go up as surely as the tide will change or the sun will rise. Keep yourself moving in harmony with the energy of Infinite Intelligence, and you will soon find yourself in that "summer" part of the cycle where the days are longer and the nights are shorter. Be patient.

Gender and Gestation

Gender: The Union of Opposites

In the union of opposites there is strength to go where neither could go alone.

Female and Male are polar opposites in many ways. Ask anyone who has been in a relationship! While it is true that women are internally focused and intuitive, many men are also reflective and sensitive to the feelings of others. Both men and women can be aggressive and overpowering. They can also be cooperative and humble. The truth is, everything in the physical world as well as in the spiritual world, is a mix of opposite characteristics. Male and female, yin and yang, inward and outward, introspective and extroverted. It is this blend which creates a whole person, a meaningful domestic union or the prosperity of an entire culture.

The Law of Gender and Gestation has to do with balance and creation. It doesn't matter if the creation is on the physical, intellectual or spiritual level. Any creation requires the balanced union of opposite forces. There is left brain and right brain, positive and negative space, subtle versus bold, ego and soul. All things in the universe are maintained in a state of balance. It is this balance of opposites that gives birth to creative intelligence.

Nature moves toward a state of balance. If you leave a cup of hot tea and a glass of ice water on the kitchen counter, a few hours later the water is at room temperature, and so is the tea. This is the Law of Entropy in action, discussed previously. Anything that is warmer than its surroundings will lose heat until it is the same temperature. If it is colder than the surrounding environment, it will gain heat – also until it is the same as the environment around it. On the larger scale of the whole earth, ocean currents, local winds and the great jet streams all move in response to the flow of energy toward balance. Heat is balanced with cold, high pressure with low pressure. All of the weather that we see every day is the result of nature moving to maintain balance. Unbalanced forces cause movement. It is important to remember this in your own life. If you have within you a feeling of unbalanced forces, it means you are in a perfect position to move. Moving into a state of balance is one of the laws of life.

It is impossible for creation to take place on the physical, mental or spiritual planes without this Law. Reproduction of a new generation of almost all forms of life, both animal and plant, require male and female cells to unite. Life on earth depends upon the Law of Gender. In the spiritual world too, the union of opposites is the basis of creation, growth and abundance.

Gender and the Rhythm of Life

Not you nor I nor anyone know
How oats, peas, beans and barley grow.

English Folk Song, c.1650

> *And God created great whales, and every living creature that moveth, which the waters brought forth abundantly, after their kind, and every winged fowl after his kind: and God saw that it was good.* – Genesis 1:21
>
> *And God said, Let the earth bring forth the living creature after his kind, cattle, and creeping thing, and beast of the earth after his kind: and it was so.* – Genesis 1:24
>
> *Male and female created he them; and blessed them… in the day when they were created.* – Genesis 5:2

The union of opposites is a fundamental driving force of life. Every living thing in both the natural and the spiritual world reproduces, and the offspring is always similar to the parents. Simple plants and animals often reproduce just by their parent cells dividing into two "daughter" cells. But for all of the higher plants and animals, reproduction requires male and female individuals to exchange DNA, from which a new generation is produced which has similarities to both the male and female parents.

For several years I gathered seeds from plants in my garden, dried them, and planted them the next spring. If I sprouted tomato seeds, I expected tomato plants similar to the plants I had grown the year before. I did not expect cabbage seeds to produce corn, or squash seeds to produce carrots or dandelions. I did find out that if I planted a seed from a Golden Delicious apple, the apple tree that grew was a wild variety that was almost inedible, but that was because I had not learned about grafting.

Reproduction produces new generations genetically similar to the parent generation. The same thing is true in the spiritual world. We are not just physical and intellectual creatures. We are spiritual beings. Like our bodies, our spirits are living things which are part of and in constant touch with Infinite Intelligence. We each have within our spiritual nature male and female components. Like the concept of yin and yang, these two opposite characteristics are unified in us, and create the balance needed to make us fully functioning spiritual beings.

Gestation, Growth, Reproduction and Death

One day suddenly becomes another, like the passing of time in a dream.

Before long, love, children, a basket full of flowers, memories,

As days flow like leaves on a rushing stream looking for its ocean.

Through it all, gratitude for the power of life, the turning of the great wheels.

One of the greatest rhythms of life is the cycle of birth, reproduction and death.

Every living thing requires time to grow and reach the point where it is able to reproduce itself. Bacteria reproduce every half hour. Some insects can reproduce only nine days after an egg is laid. In the world of mammals, mice are astonishing! They are reproductive when they are six to eight weeks old. In elephants, the time to reach reproductive age is between 11 to 20 years. The actual gestation period, from fertilization to birth, is about 20 days in mice, and nearly two years in elephants. But then, mice live less than four years, while elephants live over seventy.

Every form of life has its own cycle of maturity, gestation and life span. These many life cycles are all intertwined on the earth, and they are dependent on each other in many ways. For just one example, think of all the things that we as humans depend on that comes from the life cycle of the honeybee. Fruits and vegetables, cotton and sugar, all need bees to exist, and our lives depend on these things.

The great rhythm, from fertilization of an egg through to reproductive maturity, and finally death and the return of energy to the web of life, our life as we know it is deeply interwoven with the rhythms of all life.

> *Behold, thou hast made my days as an handbreadth; and mine age is as nothing before thee:* – Psalm 39:5
>
> *Seeing his days are determined, the number of his months are with thee, thou hast appointed his bounds that he cannot pass;* – Job 14:5
>
> *For what is your life? It is even a vapour, that appeareth for a little time, and then vanisheth away.* – James 4:14

We are fortunate to be living in a time when the life expectancy of humans is increasing. Still, every living thing takes time to mature. This is true for plants, whales and babies, as well as for goals in life. We know quite a bit about plants and babies, less about whales, and very little about the birth, growth and maturity of goals in our lives. The time it takes for a goal to mature and become productive may vary over a wide range, depending on how large or lofty the goal is, and on the desire, vision, focus, and persistence of the person within whom the goal lives. For many people, the goal that the original person envisioned has continued far beyond the time that the person was physically here on earth. For Jesus, the message that He brought has continued for a hundred generations of humans.

The Parable of the Mustard Seed describes this law in a slightly different way:

> *It (the kingdom of God) is like a grain of mustard seed, which, when it is sown in the earth, is less than all the seeds that be in the earth: But when it is sown, it groweth up, and becometh greater than all herbs, and shooteth out great branches; so that the fowls of the air may lodge under the shadow of it.* – Mark 4:30-34, Matthew 13:31-3 2, Luke 13:18-19

Seeds grow into mature plants by following the same Laws of Nature that all of creation follows, including the Laws of Gender and Gestation, and the Laws of Vibration and Attraction. That is because a tiny mustard seed, like everything else in the universe, is made of energy. A seed has a purpose built into its energy. It has within itself not only energy, but also the gift of life. Along with life is the overwhelming drive to grow. The seed has a goal to mature and reproduce itself. Because it has life, the seed, when it germinates in the moist, fertile ground, attracts to itself exactly the energy it needs from the soil. It does this by the process of chemotaxis, mentioned earlier. The seed attracts bacteria which not only carry nutrients, but enzymes which stimulate growth. The seed attracts water and the nutrients it requires. Other chemicals in the soil are not attracted or absorbed by the germinated seed.

You may have seen a photo of a beautiful little flower growing and blooming out of a crack in the concrete in some abandoned industrial site, among garbage and discarded trash. That flower took from its environment just the things it needed to grow and bloom where it was. So it is with the mustard seed. In fertile soil there is an abundance of energy to support the life of the seed and allow it to thrive. The young mustard plant will grow until it becomes "greater than all herbs," like a small tree, big enough for birds to nest in. When that time is fulfilled, the mustard plant will blossom and produce an abundance of seeds just like itself, to complete the cycle by following exactly the Laws set down by Infinite Intelligence.

If you want to see change in your life, remember the Law of Gestation. Small goals and small changes can take place within a few days or weeks. Larger goals may take more time and require more persistence, determination and focus to keep them growing. But grow they will. It is part of the Law. Just remember to be patient and keep pressing toward the mark. Everything takes time to mature and produce fruit.

PART FOUR:
ACHIEVING ABUNDANCE:
APPLYING THE LAWS

The universe will move in response to your desire, but you must also move to make room in your life to receive it.

Every person has a desire to grow, to expand, to become a better person and live an abundant, fulfilled life. This is absolutely possible. Actually it must happen if the Laws are followed, and not just for a select few who have been born into the right family or who know the right people. An abundant life is in perfect harmony with God, Infinite Intelligence, and with the spiritual Laws of Nature. Jesus himself told us many times and in many ways that we can have what we desire. Sometimes He worded things carefully so His words would only be understood by a few, but the truth is, the promise of the Laws are available to anyone who has the desire, persistence, faith and belief that Infinite Intelligence is able to give that what is desired. In fact, at the time of asking, God has already given to us the object of our desire.

In this last section we will go over the fundamentals of how the Laws can be applied in your life.

Imagine yourself walking along a well-trodden path through a wooded countryside located in a country you have never visited. You come around a corner and see a high stone wall with a large door in it. The door is closed, but you feel deep within yourself that it is very special, a door that will open you to a land of opportunity and possibility. All that you need is some way that you may unlock the door, step through it into the new land, and start walking along the path that leads to growth, abundance, and fulfilling of your purpose in life. You look down. The key is in your hand.

Expansion and Growth

Do not fear change. Embrace it. Change is growth.

> *...they (seeds) which are sown on good ground... bring forth fruit, some thirtyfold, some sixty, and some an hundred.*
> – Mark 4:20

I love to grow poppies, and not just because of their beauty or the medicinal properties of the plant. The papery petals, red or lavender, last only a few days. I love them because every year I am inspired by my poppies. A poppy seed is one of the tiniest in the plant kingdom. The seed is smaller than the head of a pin, but contained within that tiny seed is abundance. It is a living example of spiritual law.

One spring I planted seeds in a patch where I had planted poppies before. But as spring progressed, I noticed a poppy growing many yards away. A volunteer. I have no idea how the seed ended up way over there, but that poppy wanted to grow! Water, light and soil were converted into new life, with no help from me. By midsummer it was over four foot tall, robust, and had nine beautiful blossoms. As summer started to wind down, the blossoms fell off, and the seed pods grew fat. They looked like intricate little pottery jars. When they dried, I collected the seeds, like I do every year. That one plant had produced several thousand seeds, enough to fill part of a cup.

That summer I learned a lesson about what abundance means. I want to be like that volunteer poppy. I desire growth and abundance in my life. I take what I need from my surroundings, according to the natural laws, and allow Infinite Intelligence to work. Abundance is the result.

> *...God said unto them, Be fruitful, and multiply, and replenish the earth.* – Genesis 1:28

The Peach Tree

When I was in my twenties I was offered a job teaching in another state. I moved my family to a small farm not too far from the school where I would be working. The new place was just right. It was right along a river and had about four acres of pasture for grazing a cow or goats. Behind the house was a chicken house with a large pen that had been used for over a decade to keep chickens. The ground inside the chicken run was packed hard with manure that had accumulated over the years. Not a single plant lived there because the chickens ate every living thing.

We put our chickens in the chicken house. When spring came and my thoughts turned to gardening, I thought, "The chicken run is so large that I could fence off half of it and make it into a salad garden." So I did. The hard ground was surprisingly easy to turn over and had no rocks. I planted the seeds of salad vegetables, and they grew like crazy in the rich, aged chicken manure.

That salad garden was a ton of work! Since the chickens couldn't get in to patrol and eat everything that grew, the seeds of quackgrass, blackberries and other weeds also sprouted and grew prolifically. It was a chore hoeing the rows and pulling weeds that wanted to take over the lettuce, onions and carrots which I had planted.

Outside the front door of our house one morning I noticed that a young peach tree had sprouted from a peach pit in the flower bed. It was skinny, about eight inches tall, but had a few leaves. I decided to transplant it into that rich salad garden soil. It took off like a rocket! I just watered it and stood back. By the end of the summer it was almost six foot tall and bushy with dark, healthy leaves.

The next summer that tree grew taller than I could reach. It bloomed and produced not peaches but nectarines, tender, rich and juicy. I was elated, but also in a state of disbelief because fruit trees usually take several years before they produce fruit. This tree was large and productive the second season! The difference was the quality of the soil that the little "seedling had been planted in.

Inside each of us is spiritual soil in which anything that is planted will grow. The spiritual soil within us is absolutely perfect. It contains all of the energy and nutrients necessary to feed any kind of seed planted there. It is our responsibility to be careful what we plant. Seeds of doubt or fear will grow into huge plants which produce fruit of more doubt and fear. Fear and doubt will stop forward progress and clog up the entire working mechanism that result in growth and prosperity. But seeds of prosperity, gratitude, understanding, and worthy dreams will also sprout and grow. When these mature, they produce more of the same according to the Law of Gender and Gestation.

The Expanding Dream

Never be afraid to dream the biggest dream. Desire it with a burning passion. Fall in love with it, take it inside you, and make it real.

Expansion is a law of nature. Even on an everyday scale, we can witness living things growing as they take in nutrients. From plants that grow from a seed, to children and kittens growing into adults, we see evidence of expansion, of growth.

The same thing is true of our inner self. Growth is the law. Ideas are seeds of thought that are planted in the fertile soil of the mind, and they will grow. Like natural soil, any seed planted in your mind will take in energy and grow, whether it is a seed of prosperity or a seed of misery. Be careful what you allow to be planted. Tend your garden!

It has been well established that the universe is expanding. That expansion is not only huge, but it is increasing in speed every day. It's like we are all riding on a giant balloon that is inflating, and it isn't because of our place in the universe. It wouldn't matter if we lived on the far side of the universe from where we are now. If we looked around from there, the universe would also be expanding.

God, Infinite Intelligence, is the endless source of energy that results in growth and prosperity, both in the world of nature and within your life. All of the spiritual nutrients, like air and water that you require for growth, are available in infinite abundance at all times, just for the asking. If you need them, if you desire them more than anything, you will attract them to you.

As you take them in you will grow in understanding, in abundance and in wealth.

When we look around at the natural world, we see growth in every living thing. Some readers may ask, "What about the living things that get old or diseased and die?" Sure, humans, animals and plants get old and eventually pass away. That is a part of the Law of Rhythm, but growth and regeneration are part of what defines a living thing. Death and deterioration are changes in energy. Remember, nothing is lost or gained. The elements that made the living thing are given back to the earth in the great cycle of life, one of the beautiful rhythms of the physical world. The spirit, part of Infinite Intelligence, goes back to Infinite Intelligence, like the jar of ocean water pouring back into the ocean.

The nature of Infinite Intelligence is abundance. We humans, who are created in the image of God, are ourselves creators, and have the opportunity to make growth and abundance our experience by being in harmony with the nature of God and the universe, which is also part of God's creation. The only requirement is for us to focus our thoughts and our energy on expansion, growth and abundance.

Thoughts of abundance and prosperity will, like the mustard seed, attract to themselves energy which resonates in harmony with them; energy of abundance and prosperity. They have to. It's the Law of Attraction. If you focus your energy on expansion, expansion will be your experience. If you ask for growth of understanding, intuition, gratitude, belief, or any of the other positive, self-affirming qualities, those qualities will, by Law, be attracted to you because they are on the same frequency.

> *...remember the LORD thy God: for it is he that giveth thee power to get wealth, that he may establish his covenant which he sware unto thy fathers, as it is this day. - Deuteronomy 8:18*

Abundance is held out to us by God. To understand that a life of abundance is something you and I can have here on this planet, is one of the reasons Jesus lived and taught. "...it shall be given unto you; good measure, pressed down, and shaken together, and running over..."

One thing you need to tap into is faith. Faith is knowing that Infinite Intelligence has all of the energy, power and understanding necessary to fulfill the desires of any person who asks. Since God is all-powerful, it is understandable that everything you need is already available. Abundance is yours for the asking.

> *For unto every one that hath shall be given, and he shall have abundance...* – Matthew 25:29

Why Am I Here?

Purpose

To find your purpose in life, first seek your purpose. Then become your purpose.

One of the biggest questions of life is the question, "Why am I here?" That is a really good question! It is vitally important for you to know your purpose, the reason you have life on planet earth. Is it just to be born, struggle through life wondering why the things happen to you as they do, and then die? Absolutely not! Remember, we are all part of Infinite Intelligence. The kingdom of God is within you. You are a creator. Find your purpose. State your goal. Set your course.

So how to you find your purpose? There are a few steps. First, think of something you really love to do. Now think about how you can do what you really love to do, and by doing it help other people. Simple! Do what you love to do, and help other people by doing it. These are two powerful concepts. If you do what you love to do, you will never be bored or hating your work because you love to do it! It's exciting, interesting and fun. Now, make it rewarding too. Help other people by doing it. Everyone benefits. There are hundreds of ways to help other people.

I was at a high school job fair and met a girl who was sitting on an overstuffed sofa. Actually, I would call it lounging on an overstuffed sofa. I asked her if she had thought about what her purpose in life might be. "To do just what I am doing right now, but get paid for it."

I thought to myself, "Well, that's not much of a purpose, but let's see about how it could work."

The girl's vocational counsellor was sitting at her desk and said, "You can't get paid for sitting on a couch!"

That made me start thinking. I asked her, "Have you ever thought of house sitting or pet sitting?"

The girl became interested. "What's that?"

"Well," I answered, "You offer a service to watch someone's house and take care of their pets while they are gone. Most of the time you just need to be in the house, and you can sit on the couch all day with the cat in your lap if you want to. You may need to clean up the house too. Do you think you could do that?"

The girl was getting really interested. "Yes! I like cleaning anyway. People pay for that?"

"Absolutely," I replied. "When the people come home, they pay you for staying, and if you do a good job, they tell their friends, and pretty soon you are a full-time house and pet sitter. If you work it out right, you may not even need a house of your own to live in. You just go from one house to another."

"Woah!" she was excited. She looked at the counsellor, who was a little dumbfounded. "See? I told you I would be able to make money sitting on the couch!" She met the criteria. She would be doing something she loved, and in doing it, helping other people.

Every person has the ability to become aware of the great infinite reservoir of power, knowledge, understanding and abundance that is available for the asking. Any person can tap into it. This does not mean that every person is aware of this ability or of the riches that are available. The truth is, almost everyone is completely unaware of it. But Jesus took the time and made repeated efforts to make it very clear, beyond any doubt. Abundantly clear. And He said it in many ways. Jesus knew these things were very important for every person to know.

> *I am come that they might have life, and that they might have it more abundantly.* – John 10:10

The great modern teacher of spiritual laws, Earl Nightingale said, "Most people tiptoe their way through life, hoping they make it safely to death." That is a depressing way to spend something of infinite value! There is absolutely no need to spend any time in the grips of fear, tiptoeing through life, feeling like a victim, hoping to make it safely anywhere. At every step along the path, the only thing that holds you back is your own thoughts. Everything else in the universe wants you to become every bit the person that you are capable of becoming. Your purpose is first to know your purpose, then to fulfill it. There is nothing that can stand in your way because you have all the power of Infinite Intelligence just waiting for you to ask for guidance in order to achieve your purpose, to ask with the willingness to listen and respond to that guidance.

The past is something that cannot be changed. The future is full of promise. It is a blank slate upon which you can create anything you desire, for yourself and the loved ones around you. The present is a valuable gift that you can use to determine how you fill that blank slate of your future. Now is the time to find your purpose. There has never been a better time, and there is no reason to put it off any longer. There are no "buts" that should hold you back. It is true that anything is possible!

> *But seek ye first the kingdom of God, and his righteousness; and all these things shall be added unto you.* – Luke 12:33

> *...unto him that is able to do exceeding abundantly above all that we ask or think, according to the power that worketh in us...* – Ephesians 3:20

With a defined purpose, you have definite direction in life. Without a defined purpose, you are guaranteed to remain adrift and directionless, a ship without a rudder, driven by the waves and storms.

> *...let him ask in faith, nothing wavering. For he that wavereth is like a wave of the sea driven with the wind and tossed.*
> – James 1:6

Your life is full of talent. You probably know, or can remember, what those talents are. You can resurrect your talents even if you have not used them for years. If you have been using them, but only half-heartedly because of doubt or worry, you can bring them to the highest level and make yourself expand into an abundant life. You have available to you a deep reservoir of strength, wisdom and energy. What is required is faith and the will to ask.

> *And all things, whatsoever ye shall ask in prayer (faith), believing, ye shall receive.* – Matthew 21:22

Notice in the verse above that Jesus put no limit on what you can ask! Ask with faith that God has the ability to give and belief that it has already been given, and "ye shall receive." Find a purpose that you love, and a way that it will help other people. Then set your heart and mind to making it happen. God will move toward you and help you to realize your purpose.

Vision and the Path

Travel through time with your heart open and your vision clear,
And take in every new vista with gratitude.

> *Where there is no vision, the people perish:* – Proverbs 29:18

Your vision is directly related to your purpose. You probably have more than one vision. To thrive, visions must be in harmony with your purpose. For example, if your purpose is to help hungry people in India, your vision may be to be the head of a worldwide organization that brings food to villages in need. That vision would be in harmony with your purpose. If your vision was to own a motorcycle shop in Chicago, that is a fine vision, but it would not be in harmony with your purpose. Your visions must fit under the umbrella of your purpose. They must also be things that are seen some distance off. A vision is not something you can accomplish by the end of the week. It is not something that is easy to achieve. It needs to have width and scope. Think of a vision more like the view from a mountain top.

I was camping one August on the top of a mountain that looked out over a huge area of high desert. It was the time of the Perseid meteor shower. The desert was several thousand feet lower than the mountaintop I was on. In the clear, desert air, I could see for more than fifty miles, to distant mountains capped with snow. It was breathtaking. One evening, thunderclouds started to build up a ways away, down over the desert. The clouds billowed straight up until they were higher than I was. Daylight started to fade, and about the same time lightning started to flash from the inside of the thunderheads. I could see the flashes, but the clouds were so far off that there was no sound of thunder. The inside of the clouds just lit up orange with the lightning bolts, silently magnificent. Far above the clouds, an occasional meteor flashed by. The vision was clear yet far away, but its beauty and magnificence stirred me deep inside, and in the vision I could feel the power of Infinite Intelligence.

Abraham had a vision of abundance, after a time of loss, looking from where he was at the present time.

> *And the LORD said unto Abram... Lift up now thine eyes, and look from the place where thou art northward, and southward, and eastward, and westward: For all the land which thou seest, to thee will I give it... – Genesis 13:14-15*

Sometimes in our lives we seem stuck in the present. We have a goal, but don't seem to be moving toward it, no matter how hard we try. At these times, we can choose to look at our circumstances and focus on what we don't have, or we can lift up our eyes and see the possibilities, the path, from where we are right now to where we want to go. We can have vision. We choose what we focus our thoughts on. We choose the thoughts we allow to enter our mind. We choose the voice we listen to.

> *And he said, Go forth, and stand upon the mount before the LORD. And, behold, the LORD passed by, and a great and strong wind rent the mountains, and brake in pieces the rocks before the LORD; but the LORD was not in the wind: and after the wind an earthquake; but the LORD was not in the earthquake: And after the earthquake a fire; but the LORD was not in the fire: and after the fire a still small voice.*
> *– I Kings 19:11-12*

Guidance comes just when we need it. Along the path toward your vision or goal, you will come upon forks in the road. The direction you choose to go will either take you closer to your goal or farther away. It is important to choose the best route.

> *Ponder the path of thy feet... Turn not to the right hand nor to the left: – Proverbs 4:26-27*

Sometimes, at a fork in the path, what seems to be the right direction to you may make a turn that you cannot see, and lead you into a trackless wilderness or murky swamp where you will get lost if you don't do some backtracking. Choices are not always clear, but you have Infinite Intelligence on your side. You can ask for guidance, and since Infinite Intelligence is always for expansion and growth, you will receive the guidance you request.

> *And thine ears shall hear a word behind thee, saying, This is the way, walk ye in it, when ye turn to the right hand, and when ye turn to the left.* – Isaiah 30:21

> *And the LORD shall guide thee continually… and thou shalt be like a watered garden, and like a spring of water, whose waters fail not.* – Isaiah 58:11

Your path toward your vision is also the path upon which you will gain understanding, grow as a person, and receive the abundance and riches that you seek.

> *… remember… God… giveth thee power to get wealth…*
> – Deuteronomy 8:18

This is one of the forgotten promises of God. It is overlooked. God gives us power to get wealth.

Instead of seeing the promise of God to help us get wealth, one of the most misquoted verses has often been the focus of attention. The incorrect "quote" is "money is the root of all evil." This is totally false! Money is neutral. It is a medium of exchange. Nothing more. The correct quote is:

> *For the love of money is the root of all evil: which while some coveted after, they have erred from the faith, and pierced themselves through with many sorrows.* – 1 Timothy 6:10

It is true that in this example, the love is misplaced. Some people have forgotten that we should love people and use money. Instead, they love money and use people. They are greedy for more money and use unethical means to get it. Thinking in this way is what is evil, not money.

The power to get wealth is a power given to every person by God. You have within yourself the ability to ask for wealth and abundance, to be aware and look for opportunities as they are shown, and to open the doors of possibility, to create the life and the wealth which is within your power to create.

Setting Goals

Let the love of life color your dreams with richness and joy,

And give you the passion to make your dreams come true.

When you set a goal, it is not enough to merely wish for the goal to happen. You can wish all you want, but there is little chance that what you wish for will appear. You must also take some kind of action. Taking action raises your frequency of vibration and opens the channel of communication between your thoughts and Infinite Intelligence. What kind of action do you need to take?

Some day you may find yourself in a situation that just needs to change, and the only way to make the change is to move yourself to a different environment. Remember the nature of the universe is change, and change is good. Things need to be left behind and the door to the past closed in order for a new door to open. New goals can then be set. Once you have set a new goal, defined a new YOU, a vision appears on the screen of your mind. The vision is of your new goal, the person that is the new you, and the life you want for yourself. Your power of perspective allows you to judge the distance from where you are to where you want to be. You are ready to start the journey from here to there.

The apostle Paul understood two of the necessary actions needed to attain a worthy goal.

> ...*but this one thing I do, forgetting those things which are behind, and reaching forth unto those things which are before, I press toward the mark for the prize...* – Philippians 3:13-14

It is easy to let the things that are behind you, in the past, affect what you want to do here and now, in the present, to move yourself closer to the goal that you desire. To clearly focus on the goal, you need to forget the things in your past that hold you back. These may be things like feelings of unworthiness that you inherited from your parents, or the fear of ridicule from friends that you have had for years; friends who say things like,

"Who do you think you are?" Past failures or mistakes people made years ago often haunt them to this day. You need to forget those things that are behind. Your goal is not in that direction.

But listen: not all of the past needs to be forgotten. You know there are experiences in your past that were good, that taught you valuable lessons. There are people in your past who had a beneficial influence on you, who showed you the value of love or of setting worthy goals. Remember these things because they will move you forward, closer to your goal.

When you remember those who have touched your life, given you a higher purpose and made you want to be a better person, you can be thankful for that time of remembering, for that person who embraced you, and know that you are blessed.

You also will need to reach forward to that time in the future when your goal is achieved, when you have "made it," and the prize you desired is actually in your hands. Reaching forth means visualizing the goal that you seek, the good that is yours, and how that good flows through you and out to others. Think of how happy you are, how proud of yourself. Bask in the joy of accomplishment, in the sense of achievement. These positive emotional feelings will strengthen the attraction of your goal to you. Only by reaching forth, reaching for the dream that is out there in the future waiting for you to claim it and pressing toward the mark, can you ever accomplish your goal and create future memories.

One of the first actions to take on the road to achieving your goal is to clearly define your goal. Write it down with a pen and paper. Writing engages your brain, your body and your mind in a much more effective way than simply hearing, speaking or typing. This has been shown many times in learning studies. When you write your goal down, your brain is engaged in formulating the thought and in controlling the muscles of your arm, hand and fingers. In addition, as you watch the letters being formed, there is a continuous feedback loop between what you see yourself writing and your brain's assessment of the spelling, the shape of the letters, the position of the writing on the page, and so on. These multiple layers of engagement help to imbed the thoughts you write firmly in your mind, and at the same time open your creative mind.

Write your goal on a small card about the size of a credit card, one that will fit in your purse or wallet so you can look at it every day. When you write down your goal, be brief, clear and specific about it. Make it something that you have an emotional attachment to, that you love. For example, if your goal is to have a new car, remember there are many kinds of cars. Make your goal something you really want and would love driving around. A ten-year-old pickup is very different than a brand new, red Lamborghini. They are both types of cars, but one has more emotional appeal than the other. You should also write down how you will feel after you have obtained your goal. Tell yourself how happy you are now that the car is yours, and how you love the comfort of the seat, the new car smell, the steering wheel in your hands, the sound of the engine. The result of writing down your goal is that you now have something you can touch and carry around, and it is something you have made with your own ideas. You can take out your card and read your words aloud, in your own handwriting. This gets your level of vibration stepped up, and will help to move the thought of the goal toward becoming reality.

Other examples of actions which you can undertake are to make a "to-do" list of steps involved in achieving your goal, creating a "goal board" that you put things on like pictures from magazines which represent your goal, quotes which inspire you to reach your goal, or photos, drawings or even a list of words that describe your goal and how great you will feel when it is accomplished. You can also get together with people who share your passion and vision, to talk about how to make the goal happen, and repeat affirmations about how great it is now that you have achieved your goal.

The most important thing for you to do is to state what your goal is. You must not worry about how you are going to attain it. Focus on the What, not on the How. As you start to work toward achieving your goal, you will be shown how to attain that goal, one step at a time. You will not see all of the steps. The very first step is to imagine the goal and become emotionally involved with that goal. Imagine the goal already having been achieved, and take the steps toward the goal as they are shown to you, one step at a time. Be alert. Look for the next step, or maybe the next person who appears to be a "chance" meeting, who mentions something you need to know, who is on the same wavelength as you, or otherwise inspires you to move forward on your path toward your goal.

Courage, Fear and Love

A bird in flight does not fear the earth beneath.

She only focuses on the goal ahead.

Along the path toward attaining your goal, you may run into difficult stretches, what appear to be obstacles, or a sudden fork in the path, where you are not sure which way to turn. These times can cause anxiety, doubt or fear to rise up. Remember that these emotions, if you dwell on them, can stop your forward progress. Change your mind. Focus instead on the courage that is within you, your confidence in the power of Infinite Intelligence, and thoughts of abundance, prosperity and harmony with the Law.

> *For God hath not given us the spirit of fear; but of power, and of love, and of a sound mind.* – 2 Timothy 1:7

> *Be of good courage, and he shall strengthen your heart...* – Psalm 31:24

The psalmist brought out a very important concept which often is completely overlooked. "Be of good courage." Courage is part of our being. Courage is inside us.

You may have been told during some time of struggle or indecision to pray for courage. This advice was given by a well-meaning person, but unfortunately that person did not understand the nature of courage. Courage does not come from outside you, courage is something that is inside you. You can ask for support or for love, but to make a difficult decision, face something that you are afraid of, or tackle an "unsolvable" problem, you have to dig deep and find courage within yourself. Courage is determination; determination to do what is needed to make a right decision even though it goes against the opinions of others. Courage is needed to take a step in the right direction even though you are filled with fear. Courage helps you to stay on the path toward your goal when you cannot see around the next corner. Courage allows you to stand for what you know to be true, in the face of fear, doubt or criticism. Sometimes along the path of life, courage is needed to just keep on going.

> *Peace I leave with you, my peace I give unto you: not as the world giveth, give I unto you. Let not your heart be troubled, neither let it be afraid.* – John 14:27

Courage is not the absence of fear. It is going forward in the face of fear. We experience fear when the security and comfort of our life is challenged, but fear is the first step on the road to change. If you are afraid, it is a good thing because it means that change is just a few steps ahead and you are pointed in the right direction. Jesus put it very clearly:

> *And he said unto them, Why are ye so fearful? How is it that ye have no faith?* – Mark 4:40

Faith is knowing that God, Infinite Intelligence, has a deep reservoir of energy and is able to move the universe to give you what you need. To go ahead, you may need to close the door of the past behind you, open the door of opportunity in front of you, and step over the threshold. When the path ahead is unknown, these simple actions can be very scary. And there are times when to open or close a door, you may also need a key!

The Magic Key

A while ago my wife and I went into a local antique store. Sitting atop a display case was a flat, wooden box filled with old keys. Skeleton keys, they call them. The clerk said they had been bought from an old English locksmith and were over a century old. I was fascinated by the odd release patterns cut into the ends, and poked through the keys for several minutes, fascinated by the handmade intricacy of a lost art. I imagined the doors of English houses or shops that the keys once fit, the lives and possessions they protected.

A few days later I went back to the antique store, drawn by the keys. After a few more minutes of poking, I picked out four keys and took them to the clerk. She was a little surprised that I was buying four. I looked at her and explained, "There are doors along the path of life. Many of them are locked, but only need a key to open them. These are the doors of opportunity, opening to new worlds of abundance and growth. There are other doors which are standing open. These are the doors to the past. Although it is possible to enter and dwell on the other side, that is not a place of abundance or growth. These doors should be closed and locked. I want to remember this."

The clerk smiled. "So it's more than the keys."

In order to unlock the door to a new world of opportunity, often a door to the past must be closed and locked. The same key works for both.

I strung one of the keys on a cord and hung it around my neck, close to my heart. I gave one to my wife, one to my daughter, and one to a close friend. I told each of them the significance that the key had for me. A few days later, I turned in a different set of keys, the keys to my building and office at the community college where I had been teaching, and said goodbye to my dean. Up ahead, on my path in life, I knew there would be a new door that I would open with gratitude for a new chapter and a new understanding of my life.

> *There is no fear in love; but perfect love casteth out fear:*
> – 1 John 4:18

> *Fear ye not therefore, ye are of more value than many sparrows.*
> – Matthew 10:31

Fear is a powerful force. If you allow fear to work in your mind, it can and will lock up your ability to move at all. It works the same way as the medieval prison chains. You still have chains in your life. Everyone does. Even though those chains are imaginary, to your subconscious mind they are very real and just as binding as a chain and shackle driven into the stone wall of a prison cell. But again, it is important to note that I said, "If you allow" fear to work. Fear is thought energy that comes from thoughts deep in your subconscious mind. Fear has its greatest power when you are dealing with unknown factors in your future or when you are faced with things that you have been taught to fear. Fear of future events are purely imaginary, but this kind of fear has the power to attract other negative energy. Fear of things like spiders or enclosed places are the result of thoughts that have been taught to us by other people or by watching things like horror movies. These thoughts can be replaced by developing confidence, love for all things, or thinking of the safety and protection that is ours through faith in the infinite power and support of God.

> ...*And his chains fell off from his hands.* – Acts 12:7

> ...*he bringeth out those which are bound with chains.*
> – Psalm 68:6

> ...*he leads out the prisoners to prosperity*
> (English Standard Version).

Releasing the Chain

Sharen and I were in San Diego for an anniversary vacation. We rented bikes for a fun, exploratory tour of La Jolla Village and to spend time at a popular surfing beach about two miles from the hotel. The mid-October weather was surprisingly pleasant. Eighty degrees with a slight sea breeze made the short bike ride enjoyable. We stayed on the trails which followed the bluffs by the ocean, occasionally sidetracking through the quiet residential streets of this classic, southern California beach community. Along winding streets, we pedaled up hills and coasted down. The diverse trees and grounds around the homes were thoughtfully manicured. Biking was enjoyable, and the two miles went by quickly.

On the way back we decided to take a different route, which took us down a winding drive. I was leading. Up a hill and around the corner, we coasted down a long incline, right next to heavy traffic. At least I thought it was we. A ways down the hill I stopped, expecting to see Sharen close behind. She was not there. I rode back up to the last corner I had turned. No Sharen in sight. I pedaled back up the hill and found her standing next to her upside down bike. Her chain had jumped off the sprocket as she shifted down to go up the hill, and it was jammed tightly between the sprocket and the spokes. Two exposed rivets held the chain tightly in place. We started to work together in the late sunlight. She held the chain loose. I tried to turn the wheel while I pulled on the jammed chain. I caught her finger once, and she let me know it!

After some minutes we had everything free except the links that were locked behind the two rivets. No amount of pulling would budge them. Our hands were black, the sun was setting. I thought that if I had something like a screwdriver, I could pry the chain loose. But we had no tools, and our oily fingers were of no use.

Then Sharen had a flash of inspiration. "Maybe my key would work." She had the antique key which I had given her hanging around her neck. I looked at it, but it was too short and wide to fit into the space. But… I had my key, also hanging around my neck! It was longer and narrower than Sharen's. I was surprised that I hadn't thought of it. I had been too focused on the problem and the lack of a screwdriver to think of something that I already had.

I took the key off my neck. It barely fit into the space and left little room for any prying. As I held the key in place next to the chain, Sharen rotated the wheel slightly. Suddenly, the chain just slipped past one of the rivets, then the other, with none of the prying force I had envisioned. It was released! The chain was free! In another minute we had the chain back on the sprockets. We tested the pedals, and the wheel turned just like it should. Sharen got on and we rode back to the hotel, elated.

Sometimes in life we get stuck. Focusing on the stuck-ness doesn't help in getting unstuck. We find ourselves in a situation where our chain is jammed, whether it is a bike chain or some other chain of life of our own making. We are held back, stopped in our tracks. No fighting, strength or force helps. Fighting just makes the chain tighter. But often we have the very thing we need, the key, to change everything, and the key is something we already possess. We just need to think of it, and apply it to the problem. That key that locks doors behind us and opens doors in front of us, is also the key that can free chains that keep us from moving forward. When we finally use it to free the chain, we find it no longer takes a struggle. The chain just releases. Like magic.

As Sharen and I rode back, we were both so happy and grateful that in a time of potential frustration and struggle, we had learned a valuable lesson, a gift from the universe to us.

The polar opposite of fear is love. Since they are polar opposites, they cannot both exist in your mind at the same time. Only one will dominate.

Paul said, "Perfect love casts out fear." But you must choose which one you allow to dominate.

There is an old story of a wise grandparent talking with a grandchild about life. The child asked why sometimes life seems to be a struggle. The grandparent said, "Inside each of us there are two wolves. One is named Fear and the other, Love. Both of them want to control our life, but only one can dominate. When Fear is in control, it brings with it Anger, Doubt and Resentment. Together they lead us into a dark cave where we can become lost. When Love is in control, it brings with it Gratitude, Prosperity and Inspiration. Together they lead us to a place of Strength, Abundance and Light."

The child replied, "I know what you mean. When I come to a fork in the path, I can feel both of them fighting to make me choose which way to go. If they both want to dominate, which one will win?"

The grandparent looked deep into the child's eyes. "Like all creatures, these wolves are alive. They each need food. The one who will win is the one you choose to feed."

That struggle never ends. I am a grandparent. Even now, there are forks in the path, or the way is steep, rough or lost in the fog of night. Still, I choose which wolf to feed. I desire strength, abundance and light. I choose to feed Love.

...therefore love is the fulfilling of the law. – Romans 13:10

Getting Through the Rough Spots

Persistence

If you love life, dream. If you hate life, dream more.

You don't need to have sunshine to be happy. Go out and dream in the rain.

Hard work strengthens your body. It makes you weary and helps you to dream.

> *And Jesus said unto him, No man, having put his hand to the plough, and looking back, is fit for the kingdom of God.*
> *– Luke 9:62*

We all want our lives to be better, if only in small ways. Many people would like their lives to be better in bigger ways. Whether it is a nicer house, a better job, a better relationship, feeling good about yourself, or more free time to enjoy family, most of us would agree that there are places in our lives that could be changed in positive ways. Wanting a positive change is a great start, but just wanting it is not enough to make it happen. It takes effort. This effort is called persistence, which is defined as, "Firm or obstinate continuance in a course of action in spite of difficulty or opposition." When we think of it this way, it's clear that we need to infuse our "want" with determined, persistent action. Keep on keeping on.

The word "importunity" in the King James Version is defined as "determined persistence." In one explanation of the need for determined persistence to receive what we want, Jesus told this story:

> *And he said unto them, Which of you shall have a friend, and shall go unto him at midnight, and say unto him, Friend,*

> lend me three loaves; For a friend of mine in his journey is come to me, and I have nothing to set before him? And he from within shall answer and say, Trouble me not: the door is now shut, and my children are with me in bed; I cannot rise and give thee. I say unto you, Though he will not rise and give him, because he is his friend, yet because of his importunity [determined persistence] he will rise and give him as many as he needeth. And I say unto you, Ask, and it shall be given you; seek, and ye shall find; knock, and it shall be opened unto you. For every one that asketh receiveth; and he that seeketh findeth; and to him that knocketh it shall be opened.
> – Luke 11:5-10

This person had a definite need, a desire, not for himself, but in order to help another. He was not about to be sent away empty handed! There are three important points here. First, the person had a problem and a definite solution. The problem was, his guest was hungry and he had no food. The solution was at his neighbor's house. Second, he took action. He went to his neighbor's house and banged on the door. Third, he was persistent. He kept banging until he woke up his neighbor, and would not be turned away until he got what he needed to help his friend. Determined persistence is one of the keys to receiving what you need in life and to achieving any lasting change. It is essential if you expect to achieve a goal, and it is necessary for you to attain your purpose in life.

> ...let us lay aside every weight... and let us run with patience the race that is set before us... – Hebrews 12:1

Distance runners know about persistence. I coached distance runners for fifteen years. They knew about the benefits of training hard and of pushing themselves beyond what they thought possible. Every summer for several years we attended a high altitude running camp which lasted seven days. One of those days was called "The Big Day." It started at 5:30 AM, at an altitude of 9500 feet. We hiked down a big canyon to 4500 feet, around the end and back up another canyon to end up, twenty-three miles and sixteen hours later, back at camp at 7500 feet. We were cut and bruised, some with twisted ankles, and all of us were totally exhausted. But we were all back safe because no one was willing to spend the cold night out in the rocks and sage brush. Finishing that day took persistence!

On the path to your goal, you will run into places that are rough or steep, and you will want to say, "That's enough! I can't do this!" and stop. That is exactly the time you need to remember your goal, put your head down, set your mind to it, and move forward. Keep moving. Remember that the rough times strengthen you and teach you what you are capable of accomplishing. What appear to be insurmountable obstacles are actually opportunities to find new solutions, expand your vision, and grow. If things look difficult, you know you are on the right path.

Focus

As you grow, change is a constant.

Remember that change is good, and welcome it.

Struggle changes a child into an adult.

When you decide to make a change and start to take the action necessary to make the change, two forces start to work. One is the force of Infinite Intelligence that responds to your decision and your desire to change, in a positive way. God is all about growth and changes which produce expansion. After all, the universe is expanding. Everything that lives is growing, changing and reproducing.

One of the few things that stays the same or contracts is the mind of some people who are opposed to change because they don't understand that expansion and change is the nature of all life.

The second force that starts to work is within you, in your subconscious mind, where learned feelings of insecurity, inadequacy, fear and doubt lurk. These are negative thoughts that tell us, "You don't need to change. Everything is fine as it is" or "Who do you think you are? What will your friends say?" or "You are a failure! What will everyone think when you fail again?" Once a decision is made to move forward and make the change, "putting your hand to the plow," that decision needs to followed up with commitment, focus and determination. When the negative voice in your mind tries to turn you around, to look back, remind yourself that you have started in the right direction and just need to set the plough blade. It's time to turn up some new soil and get ready to plant new seeds!

To get from where you are to where you want to be, you need to stay focused. The attention span of humans has shrunk over time, mostly due to television and social media, so that now we jump from thought to thought every few seconds. It is nearly impossible for some people to concentrate on a single topic for even two minutes. Focus is very important in achieving success.

Try this two-part focusing exercise sometime. In my science classes I used it as the opening experiment at the beginning of each year. The first part of the "experiment" was an exercise in observation. The second part concentrated on the power of focus. First, sit in a comfortable chair at the kitchen table with a piece of paper, a pen and a candle in front of you. Any candle will work, whether it is a tall, red one or a flat votive candle. Light the candle and set a timer for five minutes. Silently observe the candle without letting other thoughts enter your mind. Focus on the candle with the intention of seeing and feeling how the flame behaves as the candle burns. Write down what you observe.

This part seems very simple, but is actually quite difficult. When you notice anything, even the simplest thing, write it down. There are dozens of subtle details that you can come up with. The list you make is a list of the physical properties of the burning candle. In five minutes you have learned, through your own observation, details about burning, light and heat, and gained physical knowledge.

Now the second part comes. It is both simpler and harder than the first part.

Reset the timer for another five minutes. Now try to keep your mind completely clear and focus on the non-physical qualities of the burning candle. Again, keep your thoughts focused just on the burning, the light, the candle. It may be very difficult to keep your mind absolutely clear of any thoughts, any at all, until you practice it over and over. You may be surprised at the ridiculous and trivial chatter of thoughts that will come to your mind. Do not allow yourself to be distracted. If you find you have let your mind wander, following some random thought down the rabbit hole, reset the timer and start over.

If you work at it, soon you will be able to set the timer to longer intervals, and you will be surprised at the change in your ability to focus on thoughts that will help you to grow instead of letting meaningless thoughts distract you. You will gain insight into your own spiritual nature and the spiritual nature of Infinite Intelligence.

Because focus is not practiced, things like listening to a lecture, reading a book, or meditating to clear your mind become huge, painful tasks. We all know someone (maybe yourself!) who starts a project, gets distracted, starts another project, and the first one just sits, never finished because of lack of focus. To make positive change requires focus.

For as he thinketh in his heart, so is he: – Proverbs 23:7

It has been said that we become what we spend the most time thinking about. This is true and can be seen in the accomplishments of people who have risen to the top of their calling in life, whether they are world class athletes, business leaders, inspirational speakers, doctors, artists or any one of hundreds of vocations. These are people who have devoted their thoughts and energy, their very lives, day after day, thousands of hours, with a focused goal in mind. They have made themselves experts and are recognized as such by others in their area of expertise.

In order to create something magnificent with your own body and energy requires focus on a goal. That goal needs to dominate the thoughts in your life in order to for you to achieve it.

When you have a dream that becomes a goal and you focus on that goal, something magical begins to happen. You begin to change. Your thoughts change as you focus on your goal. Your likes and dislikes begin to change because you are becoming in harmony with the goal you desire. You stop hanging out with people who have negative attitudes or who make fun of you because of your new goal. They might call you unrealistic, dreamer, naïve. And as your thoughts change, your view of the world around you changes. Your perspective changes. You begin to see opportunities where there were none before. The world starts to open up. You feel stronger, directed, optimistic.

Remember, "You are the captain of your ship. You are the master of your destiny."

Focus also means that you have your vision directed toward your goal. An analogy is often made of the captain of a ship leaving port. The captain knows the destination, and from the time the ship leaves port, the captain is focused on the destination. Assuming the ship is in good mechanical condition, the captain can make minor adjustments in the compass heading during the voyage to be certain the ship is on track.

I did a little figuring. Imagine this. Think of a captain steering a ship from Tokyo, heading for San Francisco. The captain would know that the port of San Francisco is five thousand one hundred fifty-four miles away, and the trip will take twenty-one days, give or take a little due to weather. The captain sets the compass toward San Francisco, but is off by one degree. Only one degree. That sounds like hardly anything, but if the captain does not correct this tiny error, by the time the ship gets to the west coast of California, it will be off by ninety miles! The captain won't even see the entrance to San Francisco Bay, and will end up somewhere along the rocky coast.

We need not only focus, but constant checking of where we are on the path toward our goal in life. We need to ask ourselves if we are on track and make corrections when we find that we have misjudged where we are. A tiny difference in direction adds up over a long journey.

Create the Image Then Make It Real

Create the image in your mind of the person you want to become or have a clear image of your goal. You need to focus on this image until it is crystal clear. Focusing on a clear image creates a pattern or a model in your subconscious mind toward which your creative mind and the universe can work.

Only by having a clear and precise image can the object ever take form in the world. There are many examples of this in the physical world. One of these examples has to do with creating jewelry out of precious metal.

When I was in college I studied metalsmithing as a creative release from the tedious study of graduate level physics and math. Metalsmithing is an art with which few people have had hands-on experience. In this craft, the metalsmith creates something of artistic value, like a gold ring or bronze statue, or a useful, strong and long-lasting item like a gold crown to replace a damaged tooth. The process is similar for either of these finished products.

The first requirement is an idea. A thought must be changed into an exact image, an idea, which can be made in three-dimensional form. In the case of a large statue, many drawings might be made showing different views of the finished piece before a model is constructed. In the case of a ring or small statue, a wax model is made of the exact item the artist wants to produce. This is the image, but is not the goal.

I was interested in making small animals to give away as gifts, so I started with a little bunny, moved on to a bear, and then to a duck with its wings spread, ready to land on a lake.

First I made a wax model. It was small enough that I could hold it in the palm of my hand. The wax was somewhat pliable, but I could also carve it. If I made a mistake, it wasn't like wood carving where the mistake was permanent. I could just melt some new wax and stick it on to fill in the mistake.

The wax model, when it is finished, is exactly the same as the finished piece, down to the smallest detail. But it needs to be changed from a wax model into a work of metal. This transformation process is essentially important. The procedure that makes the transformation is called lost wax casting.

The first step in the transformation is to make the wax model into a mold, into which molten metal can be poured to make a cast. The casting process produces a metal replica of the original wax model. A special kind of plaster is used, called investment plaster. Investment plaster is very fine-grained, sets up quickly, and is not affected by the high temperature of the molten metal after it dries completely. Investment plaster looks a little like flour and can easily be mixed with water to form a slurry the consistency of thick pancake batter. The word "investment" as it is used here is worth some reflection. What kind of investment are you putting around the image of your goal?

The investment plaster is painted onto the wax model with a soft artist's brush. Care must be taken to fill in every tiny crevice in the model in order to produce an exact replica. Layer upon layer of plaster is applied until the wax is completely covered and looks like a bloated blob that bears little resemblance to the original model. The blob is placed into a can filled with the slurry of investment plaster, with just the tip sticking out of the open end of the can.

Once the plaster in the can is completely dry, it is placed into a kiln upside down. As the model heats up, the wax melts and runs out of the open end, leaving a hollow shape inside, the exact shape of the original model. This is the mold. The wax is gone – hence the name "lost wax" casting. Now the mold can be used to make the final cast.

The metal to be used for the casting is placed into a ceramic bowl called a crucible, and heated with a hot flame like a welding torch until the metal melts. The melting point is different for different metals. Pewter has a relatively low melting point, about 450°F. Gold has a much higher melting point, 1948°F.

When the metal reaches its melting point, it turns into a shiny liquid that looks like mercury from an old-fashioned thermometer. Tiny fragments of black debris, called dross, float to the surface and must be skimmed off or the final product will have flaws. When the dross is removed, the metal is said to be purged or refined. Gold which has been through this process is called fine gold. Even today, the degree of refining is stamped on gold bullion, something like ".999 fine."

> *Take away the dross from the silver, and there shall come forth a vessel for the finer (metalsmith).* – Proverbs 25:4

> *And he shall sit as a refiner and purifier of silver: and he shall purify the sons of Levi, and purge them as gold and silver.* – Malachi 3:3

To make the cast, the molten metal must be poured into the mold. The pouring process is called casting. If the metal has a low melting point, it can be simply poured from the crucible into the mold. The metal finds its way into all the nooks and crannies of the mold, and will produce a replica of the original wax model. There is a challenge with metals with higher melting points because the metal solidifies as soon as the heat is removed and may not fill all the details of the mold. This challenge is solved by using a spring-loaded centrifuge with an arm that holds the crucible and the mold. The centrifuge releases like an arrow from a powerful bow when the lever is released. The spinning centrifuge arm throws or "casts" the molten metal quickly into the mold. The metal fills the mold completely before it has a chance to cool and solidify.

To finish the process, the investment plaster is removed from the cast and the final piece of art is polished. The goal, a work of art formed in precious metal, is achieved.

I love Psalm 19:7-10, which has been made into a lovely hymn, with the last verse, describing fine gold, as the chorus:

> *The law of the LORD is perfect, converting the soul: the testimony of the LORD is sure, making wise the simple.*
>
> *The statutes of the LORD are right, rejoicing the heart: the commandment of the LORD is pure, enlightening the eyes.*
>
> *The fear of the LORD is clean, enduring for ever: the judgments of the LORD are true and righteous altogether.*
>
> *More to be desired are they than gold, yea, than much fine gold: sweeter also than honey and the honeycomb.*

If you want an idea to become real, first fall in love with it. Really fall in love with your idea. Create an image then take the steps to change the image into a precious work of art.

We become what we think about. An image is created in our thoughts and begins to take form. If you want to become a successful person, you need to think thoughts of success, prosperity, abundance. If your goal is to travel to a foreign land, fill your thoughts with images of the place you want to visit and wrap those images in good emotions. Think of how excited you are to be in this new place, how happy you are to be surrounded with the colors and people. Or think of how fun it is to explore the mountains, beaches, ancient ruins, or the exciting city streets. Bathing your images in positive emotion will open the channels of communication with Infinite Intelligence and facilitate the attraction of positive creative energy into your life.

> *Finally, brethren, whatsoever things are true, whatsoever things are honest, whatsoever things are just, whatsoever things are pure, whatsoever things are lovely, whatsoever things are of good report; if there be any virtue, and if there be any praise, think on these things. – Philippians 4:8*

But seek ye first the kingdom of God, and his righteousness; and all these things shall be added unto you. – Matthew 6:33

Wisdom is the principal thing; therefore get wisdom: and with all thy getting get understanding. Proverbs 4:7

Repetition

Practice is the common denominator of all who have achieved greatness in any calling. Practice tunes the body and eliminates uncertainty from the mind.

To get a thought or idea impressed permanently in your mind takes repetition. This is how you learn any skill or new language. When toddlers learn to talk, they are learning a brand new language. They have heard their parents or siblings using this unknown language and have a sense about the emotions associated with certain phrases. But as they begin to form words, repetition becomes necessary. A parent may hold up a blue toy, get the child's attention on the toy and say, "Blue," over and over. Eventually, the child will say something like, "Boo!" The parent is overjoyed at this response and will enthusiastically tell the spouse, friends, and maybe even the checker at the grocery store.

You have probably used flash cards to help you learn translations of words if you want to learn a language, solve math problems, or learn definitions of words in a new profession. Flash cards are repetition. Repetition is a critical part of the mechanism of memorization, and it is how we learned to write the alphabet, read simple words and learn arithmetic. Repetition helps to drive new thoughts into our subconscious mind where it can be stored and become a learned behavior, a habit. Habits are behaviors which we have been repeated so many times that we no longer have to think about them. Once you learn that three times eight equals twenty-four, you don't have to think about it. You just seem to "know" that three times eight equals twenty-four, although you learned it by repetition.

The same process works for any thought or idea that you want to make into a habit. You can actually change the way you think by telling yourself over and over a new idea, goal or a quality of character that you wish to achieve. If you want to increase your trust in the care and guidance of God, you may memorize and repeat Psalm 23:

The LORD is my shepherd; I shall not want.

He maketh me to lie down in green pastures: he leadeth me beside the still waters.

He restoreth my soul: he leadeth me in the paths of righteousness for his name's sake.

Yea, though I walk through the valley of the shadow of death, I will fear no evil: for thou art with me; thy rod and thy staff they comfort me.

Thou preparest a table before me in the presence of mine enemies: thou anointest my head with oil; my cup runneth over.

Surely goodness and mercy shall follow me all the days of my life: and I will dwell in the house of the LORD for ever.

This Psalm is a series of affirmations which, if repeated, memorized and imbedded into your subconscious mind, will change your behavior and your view of the world.

One additional word: in order to make the thought really become a part of your subconscious mind, it must be accompanied by strong emotion. Some of the most powerful emotions which have the ability to make the new thought stick in your subconscious mind are love, gratitude, faith and belief. To get in tune with one of these emotions, think of yourself lying down in that green pasture. Think of how good you feel. You are comfortable, warm, secure, calm, looking up into the blue sky, grateful to be alive. You feel great! By combining that feeling of gratitude and deep contentment with the thought expressed in the opening verse of the Psalm, you will help the thought of peace and calmness become firmly fixed in your mind. It will help you remember it and recall it in the future. It will become a habit, a part of your subconscious mind. You will, without having to think about it, see the world from the perspective of a calm person.

The verses in Matthew 6:9-13, often called "The Lord's Prayer," is another example that Jesus gave as an affirmation of faith, as well as a way to ask for spiritual strength, along with trust and acceptance of others.

After this manner therefore pray ye:

> *Our Father which art in heaven, Hallowed be thy name.*
>
> *Thy kingdom come. Thy will be done in earth, as it is in heaven.*
>
> *Give us this day our daily bread.*
>
> *And forgive us our debts, as we forgive our debtors.*
>
> *And lead us not into temptation, but deliver us from evil: For thine is the kingdom, and the power, and the glory, for ever. Amen.*

Affirmations are statements you make to yourself about the person you intend to become. Repeating affirmations, if they resonate with you on a deep emotional level, can change the way you think about yourself and your place in the world. Affirmations can actually begin to create the ideal person you intend to be. Some kinds of affirmations are also called prayer and become a part of your subconscious mind by repetition.

> *Pray without ceasing.* – I Thessalonians 5:17
>
> *And he spake a parable unto them to this end, that men ought always to pray, and not to faint…* – Luke 18:1
>
> *… pray to thy Father which is in secret, and thy Father which seeth in secret shall reward thee openly.* – Matthew 6:6

The Power of Gratitude, Love and Giving Back

Gratitude

There are few qualities of character more powerful or more appealing than gratitude.

Live your love. Live your gratitude, remembering that the more you pour out, the more you have.

Giving thanks always for all things... – Ephesians 5:20

First, a little history. It is interesting that the word "gratitude" does not appear in the King James Version of the Bible, nor does the word "grateful." This is probably because "gratitude" did not appear in the English language until around 1560, only 51 years before the first publication of the King James Version. Even Shakespeare, writing at the same time in 1611, used the word "thankfulness" instead of "gratitude."

The Greek word *charis* (χάρις) was translated at that time as "thanks" or "grace." The modern Oxford English dictionary defines grace as "the free and unmerited favour of God" to humans. In more modern Bible translations the word "gratitude" is often preferred over "grace." We still use the word "grace" with the King James meaning when we sit down to eat a meal to express our gratitude. It is also interesting that the word *charis* is the root word for charisma, and for the *eucharist*, the feast of gratitude, commemorating the Last Supper.

Gratitude has been called "the heart of the Gospel" (*Journal of Psychology and Christianity* 24.2. 2005), and for a good reason. The emotion or feeling of gratitude permeates the teachings of Jesus and shows clearly in the attitudes and writings of the Apostles. Gratitude is one of the most powerful of the positive emotions because it can open a direct channel between the human mind and the mind of God, Infinite Intelligence. It is indeed one of the keys to the Universe, to understanding and love.

> *In every thing give thanks: for this is the will of God in Christ Jesus concerning you.* – 1 Thessalonians 5:18
>
> *Let the word of Christ dwell in you richly in all wisdom; teaching and admonishing one another ... singing with grace (gratitude) in your hearts...* – Colossians 3:16
>
> *...which God hath created to be received with thanksgiving (gratitude) of them which believe and know the truth.* – 1 Timothy 4:3

Possibly the most powerful phrase in any language is the phrase which in English is translated as "Thank you!" Other than the sound of a person's own name, this phrase is valued as much as a wrapped gift or even a paycheck. When it is said eye to eye with genuine gratitude, true magic takes place. People are bonded and elevated to a higher level of awareness. Self-worth is heightened, and a warm feeling of the value of life is gained. It is a phrase that is often neglected or spoken without any feeling. But when it is said in earnest, lives can be changed. Gratitude dispels fear and doubt, neutralizes anger, and even helps a person to embrace, with thankfulness, the end of physical life.

Love

And what is this thing that we call love?

The secret of the water of life

Made clear by giving, receiving

> *A new commandment I give you: Love one another. As I have loved you, so also you must love one another.* – John 13:34

This is a difficult subject to expand upon. The apostle Paul wrote the exemplary description of the power of love:

Though I speak with the tongues of men and of angels, and have not charity, I am become as sounding brass, or a tinkling cymbal. And though I have the gift of prophecy, and understand all mysteries, and all knowledge; and though I have all faith, so that I could remove mountains, and have not charity, I am nothing. And though I bestow all my goods to feed the poor, and though I give my body to be burned, and have not charity, it profiteth me nothing.

Charity suffereth long, and is kind; charity envieth not; charity vaunteth not itself, is not puffed up, Doth not behave itself unseemly, seeketh not her own, is not easily provoked, thinketh no evil; Rejoiceth not in iniquity, but rejoiceth in the truth; Beareth all things, believeth all things, hopeth all things, endureth all things.

Charity never faileth: but whether there be prophecies, they shall fail; whether there be tongues, they shall cease; whether there be knowledge, it shall vanish away. For we know in part, and we prophesy in part. But when that which is perfect is come, then that which is in part shall be done away. When I was a child, I spake as a child, I understood as a child, I thought as a child: but when I became a man, I put away childish things. For now we see through a glass, darkly; but then face to face: now I know in part; but then shall I know even as also I am known. And now abideth faith, hope, charity, these three; but the greatest of these is charity.
– 1 Corinthians 13

The Greek word *agape* (ἀγάπη) was translated as *charity* in 1 Corinthians 13. In almost every modern translation, agape is translated as "love," with the idea that it means "the unconditional love of one person toward others." This can be expanded to include human love toward God and God's love toward humans, but the important thing is that it is unconditional. The word "charity" as we generally use it today would be the Greek word *filantropia*, philanthropic love. I would encourage you to reread the verses above, with the words "unconditional love toward others" in the place of "charity." Doing this helps me to see the importance of unconditional love toward others in every aspect of my life, and to use it as a measure of my love and my commitment to make the world a better place.

And Jesus answered him, The first of all the commandments is, Hear, O Israel; The Lord our God is one Lord: And thou shalt love the Lord thy God with all thy heart, and with all thy soul, and with all thy mind, and with all thy strength: this is the first commandment. And the second is like, namely this, Thou shalt love thy neighbour as thyself. There is none other commandment greater than these. – Mark 12:29-31

Jesus said unto him, Thou shalt love the Lord thy God with all thy heart, and with all thy soul, and with all thy mind. This is the first and great commandment. And the second is like unto it, Thou shalt love thy neighbour as thyself. On these two commandments hang all the law and the prophets. – Matthew 22:37-40

Giving Back

Give with grace, receive with gratitude, and give back. This is the natural cycle, which must be followed for true fulfillment of any purpose.

...remember the words of the Lord Jesus, how he said, It is more blessed to give than to receive. – Acts 20:35

The act of giving, especially in a spirit of gratitude and love, starts a cause and effect cycle which is wonderful. Willingly giving back a portion of what has been given to us is not only satisfying, it brings us into resonant harmony with the creative energy of Infinite Intelligence. It increases our level of vibration, fills our being with positive energy, and opens doors in our life that no other action can. This has always been true.

In the Old Testament, the prophet Malachi understood the vast return offered to those who gave in a spirit of gratitude.

Bring ye all the tithes (offerings of gratitude) into the storehouse, that there may be meat in mine house, and prove me now herewith, saith the LORD of hosts, if I will not open you the windows of heaven, and pour you out a blessing, that there shall not be room enough to receive it. – Malachi 3:10

Jesus made the benefits of giving back very personal.

Then shall the King say unto them on his right hand, Come, ye blessed of my Father, inherit the kingdom prepared for you from the foundation of the world: For I was an hungred, and ye gave me meat: I was thirsty, and ye gave me drink: I was a stranger, and ye took me in: Naked, and ye clothed me: I was sick, and ye visited me: I was in prison, and ye came unto me. Then shall the righteous answer him, saying, Lord, when saw we thee an hungered, and fed thee? or thirsty, and gave thee drink? When saw we thee a stranger, and took thee in? or naked, and clothed thee? Or when saw we thee sick, or in prison, and came unto thee? And the King shall answer and say unto them, Verily I say unto you, Inasmuch as ye have done it unto one of the least of these my brethren, ye have done it unto me. – Matthew 25:34-40

One of the secrets of gaining riches in abundance is first giving. Giving is not just done after abundance is attained, it is a prerequisite to receiving abundance. And it is not to be done with the expectation of getting something in return. That is called "trading."

Give, and it shall be given unto you; good measure, pressed down, and shaken together, and running over, shall men give into your bosom. For with the same measure that ye mete withal it shall be measured to you again. – Luke 6:38

Opportunity

The greatest secrets are not really secrets at all, but things merely camouflaged, hidden in the commonplace, in plain sight.

Two sides of the property we live on border an undeveloped state park densely covered with Sitka spruce and plants native to the coastal Oregon rain forest. Trails have been cut through in winding paths, which Sharen and I often hike, to lookout points over the ocean. We value the ability to leave the everyday world behind for the energy of breaking waves and sea winds in the forest.

A few days ago, as we walked along one of the paths, I saw a fleeting glimpse of a bird flying across the path in front of me. A Fox Sparrow. A few dozen yards later, another startled bird flew out of the brush and landed in a nearby bush. A Swainson's Thrush. They appeared for only a second and flashed across the path with a flurry, but they could be identified by their coloring and flight.

In the quiet of the forest, both birds took on a deeper significance. They were, to me, visions of opportunities.

Opportunities don't come often. When they come, they are fleeting things that can be easily missed because they do not appear with a flash of color or any kind of announcement. They may even be camouflaged with the surroundings, hidden in plain sight. When they do appear, opportunities don't stick around. They require awareness. Across our peripheral vision, a quick blur of motion. It is a challenge just to see them for a split second and identify them. They can be overlooked, even ignored. When that happens, they are gone as quickly and silently as they appeared.

Like all of us, I walk my path of life, and that path also has its twists and rough spots. As I go through each day with its potential distractions, I want to stay aware and focused. I want to see opportunities when they flash across my vision, identify them, and quickly move to take advantage of the open door they represent because it is a door to understanding, growth, and expansion.

The Power of Faith, Belief and Expectation

Faith and Belief

Have faith in God's ability, belief in God's willingness and expectation that God has already done it.

Now set your heart and your soul to seek... – 1 Chronicles 22:19

Faith and belief are two qualities that are ephemeral in nature. They are wispy and formless, difficult to define, and different for different people. They are like thoughts. Although they seem on the surface to be insubstantial and weak, like thoughts, they are powerful. Very powerful! They are essential if we want to transform desire into its physical equivalent.

Faith and belief are like oil on the working mechanisms of Infinite Intelligence. They cut down the resistance of the great turning wheels of the universe, and make it easier for the law of attraction to work. They grease the hinges on the doors of heaven so the doors can open wide and abundance can be poured out into our lives. Without faith and belief, I could never see my vision or reach out and take hold of my goal. But with them, I can see clearly, beyond the horizon, and grasp the reality that is my purpose.

It is amazing to me that all of the great teachers have said the same thing. Jesus, Buddha, Mohammed, Paul. I draw near to God (or Infinite Intelligence, Cosmic Consciousness, Source, Spirit...), and God draws near to me. This is made possible through the power of faith. When I ask (pray) for what I most desire, I must believe that I will receive in order to make it so. And it's receive, in the present tense, not will receive or may receive, but receive. Present tense! It is. Energy IS. God IS.

Everyone has goals. All of us have dreams of a better life. I don't know what your dream of a better life would be, but I would guess that it includes prosperity, happiness, a fulfilling relationship, and the ability to give to others, to lift them up or help them to attain their own dreams.

Just wishing for something is not enough. There are a few other things that you need to do to set the Law of Attraction in motion and begin the moving of the universe toward you.

First, your dream must be focused into a burning desire that you think about all the time. You become what you think about. Remember that all things require an input of energy to grow or maintain stability. In order to change from a lower state of energy to a higher state, like the earlier example of water turning into steam, a much greater amount of energy must be put into the water than the energy required to merely raise the temperature. Remember that it takes five hundred times more energy to change water to steam than it takes to raise the temperature that last degree to the boiling point. Dreams, too, require focused energy if they are to have any hope of transforming into reality. This is because you are, by your creative energy, changing the state of the energy involved. You are changing water into steam, in the spiritual sense.

Part of this is done by intense emotion, and part of the magic comes from being in harmony with the object of your desire. The principle is much like the microwave oven heating water, or the tuning of guitar strings described earlier. Your thought energy must be on the same wavelength as the thing you desire. You have to be in sync, with your thoughts in the same frequency as what you desire. This harmony between your thoughts and the thing you desire will cause the Law of Attraction to begin to take effect. This is where belief becomes necessary.

Second, you must attach strong emotion to that desire. Emotion is the accelerator, it is the energy for the turning of the gears, and it makes things move in the universe. Your goal needs to be wrapped in emotion! Only then will it be accepted by your subconscious mind and kept there. The emotion you use should be a positive emotion like gratitude, prayer, enthusiasm, love, or something like the intensity of desire you feel when you really, really want something. Think of the desire that you have when you try to win the love of a person you are attracted to, or the feeling you get when you think of that car that you love, a beautiful new home or a dream vacation to a place where you have always wanted to go. That is the level of emotion that must be in your heart and mind.

> *He staggered not at the promise of God through unbelief; but was strong in faith, giving glory to God; And being fully persuaded that, what he had promised, he was able also to perform. And therefore it was imputed to him for righteousness.*
> – Romans 4:20-22

Third, you must have faith. Faith is being absolutely sure that God, Infinite Intelligence, is able to give you what you desire. That part should be easy! After all, God is infinite, omniscient, omnipresent, and is the sum of all of the energy and knowledge in the entire universe! Of course God is able to give you what you desire! Not only is God, Infinite Intelligence, able to give you what you desire, when you express your desire with faith that Infinite Intelligence is able to provide, you can relax because you have started the universe to move down a path where it is guaranteed to happen, by Law! The promise is real, and has been for over two thousand years. There are many verses which say this.

> *Now faith is the substance of things hoped for, the evidence of things not seen.* – Hebrews 11:1

> *…and when he saw her, he said, Daughter, be of good comfort; thy faith hath made thee whole. And the woman was made whole from that hour.* – Matthew 9:22

> *…Jesus beheld them, and said unto them, With men this is impossible; but with God all things are possible.* – Matthew 19:26, Mark 10:27

> *…Fear not: believe only, and she shall be made whole.*
> – Luke 8:50

> *For with God nothing shall be impossible.* – Luke 1:37

> *Jesus saith unto them, Believe ye that I am able to do this? They said unto him, Yea, Lord. Then touched he their eyes, saying, According to your faith be it unto you. And their eyes were opened.* – Matthew 9:28-30

The fourth part is totally in your own control. That part is belief. Belief is a little different than faith. Faith means knowing Infinite Intelligence is able to give what you desire. Belief means accepting the fact that Infinite Intelligence is not only able to give you that which you desire, but has *already given* to you that for which you have asked. At the very moment you ask, believing, your request has started to move into form. Not sometime in the future. It is already done! In one instance, the person who was being healed was not even present, but her father's desire to have her healed, mixed with belief, started the process of fulfilling the desire immediately, from miles away.

> *Jesus said unto him, If thou canst believe, all things are possible to him that believeth.* – Mark 9:23
>
> *Be not afraid, only believe.* – Mark 5:36
>
> *…when Jesus heard it, he answered him, saying, Fear not: believe only, and she shall be made whole.* – Luke 8:50
>
> *…I know whom I have believed, and am persuaded that he is able…* – 2 Timothy 1:12

Jesus was not talking about something imaginary or something only in the spiritual sense. Nor was he speaking figuratively or using analogy. He was saying some of the statements above while He was in the act of healing people. In fact, Jesus went on to be more clear in case some of those listening didn't get it:

> *And all things, whatsoever ye shall ask in prayer, believing, ye shall receive.* – Matthew 21:22

There is no limit to the ability of God, Infinite Intelligence, to give you the thing you desire. God is infinite. And Jesus made it very clear. "What things soever ye desire," "And all things, whatsoever ye shall ask in prayer, believing." He could not have been more clear! The only condition placed on the fulfillment of desire is that you must completely believe that you have received the object of your desire. This is a great secret that has been hidden in plain sight for thousands of years. The only thing that stands in the way of fulfillment of desire, attaining a goal or fulfilling your purpose in life, prosperity and abundance, is belief. It is a wonderful thing that Jesus was consistently literal in the explanation of how Infinite Intelligence works, yet we often overlook the obvious.

We attract into our lives the things that we think about most. Over time, our perception of the world changes and we actually become what we think about. A person who really wants to become a musician, if she or he applies thought, will and action, will improve and become a better musician. A person who is interested in history, who studies, thinks and reads, will become, at some level, a historian. Although people may not all rise to the pinnacle of expertise or proficiency, every person who is considered the best in their area continually focus time, thought and effort toward their passion to become really great. This gift is available to all of us. Some people call it daydreaming or meditation or studying. Others call it the power of prayer.

When I am really fascinated by some new idea or possibility, I let my mind wander. Often I end up in a future where the object of my fascination is real and is actually mine. I have friends who have had these kinds of visionary daydreams about a better job. By seeing themselves in the future with the new job, the possibility of that dream job actually becoming a part of their future actually increases. God, Infinite Intelligence, sees the desires of our hearts, and if we have faith in the power of Infinite Intelligence to move the wheels of the universe, energy can be shifted to make the thought, the image, the desire of the heart, become real.

Think of this. The "electronic computer" was just an idea in 1935. Two years later a simple machine made with telephone relays was able to add numbers. Within thirty years, the idea had become a huge machine that filled an entire room. This computer was capable of performing advanced engineering calculations. Twenty more years saw the dawn of the "personal computer" age, when Steve Jobs turned his idea into the Apple (and later the Macintosh) computer, and Michael Dell made his computer company a household name.

Today, many people carry a phone in their pocket which is a computer more powerful than the giant computers of the 1950s. These machines can send a video to someone on the other side of the planet, recognize your voice and talk back to you, and answer almost any question you ask. And you can use your phone to talk with several people at the same time while you see them, wherever they are on the earth. Talk about an idea becoming real! There is absolutely no limit to what you may ask!

Jesus answered and said unto them, Verily I say unto you, If ye have faith, and doubt not, ye shall not only do this which is done to the fig tree, but also if ye shall say unto this mountain, Be thou removed, and be thou cast into the sea; it shall be done. – Matthew 21:21

There is an old story about a cowboy in the American southwest back in the "Wild West" days who was riding alone across a hot, dry desert where the only living thing was prickly cactus. The sun was blistering, and the cowboy was out of water for himself and his horse. In the middle of the heat of the day, when it seemed like there was no hope for any water to quench his thirst, he saw a water pump there in the desert.

He thought he was imagining things until he got off his horse and touched it. The pump was an old cast iron type, meant to be operated by hand. He knew about these pumps. They had a washer inside made of leather that only worked when the leather had been allowed to soak up water and swell to make a seal. He tried pumping on the iron handle, but there was no water. Then he saw an old metal can that had once contained baking powder under a nearby rock. He opened the can and found a brown piece of paper, folded, with a note. It was a little poem, humorously written in pencil in a scratchy hand. It had been written by an old prospector, probably long gone. The note said,

> This pump is old, but she works.
> So give'er a try.
> I put a new sucker washer in her.
> You may find the leather dry.
> You've got to prime the pump, and wait a bit.
> Then work that handle like there's a fire.
>
> Under the rock you'll find some water
>
> Left there in a bitter's jar.
> Now there's just enough to prime it with,
> So don't you go drinkin' first.
> Just pour it in and pump like mad
>
> And, Buddy, you'll quench your thirst.

You've got to prime the pump.
You must have faith, and believe.
You've got to give of yourself

Before you're worthy to receive.

Drink all the water you can hold.
Wash your face, cool your feet.
But leave the bottle full for others.
Thank you kindly,

Desert Pete

The cowboy looked around and found the jar under the rock, just like the poem said. It was nearly a quart and would have helped him to get the rest of the way across the desert. Should he drink it or do as the poem said? "You must have faith and believe, You've got to give of yourself…"

For some reason the cowboy trusted the old poem and poured the water into the pump to prime the leather washer. He waited for what seemed like hours, but was only a few minutes. Then he started pumping again, and could hear the gurgling of water deep in the ground beneath the pump. Soon there was a gushing of cool, clear water! The cowboy drank, soaked his hat and hair, and the horse drank his fill too. Before he left to finish his journey, the cowboy remembered to refill the jar and replace the note so the next thirsty traveler could benefit from the good work of Desert Pete.

As I journey along this path I have chosen, I sometimes find myself in a situation like the cowboy. But "like a bolt out of the blue" the pump appears, an unexpected and maybe illogical solution. To make it more of a challenge, I have to make a choice. Do I trust the "poem," or just take the quick solution that's in my hand? By taking the quick solution, I turn my back on the really meaningful and fulfilling potential that is offered. Some call it a leap of faith. I don't know how, but I know the voice that guides me. I choose trust and faith, and release all of the arguments of my logical mind. Pour in the water and start pumping!

Poem from Desert Pete, courtesy of Billy Edd Wheeler

> *... verily I say unto you, If ye have faith as a grain of mustard seed, ye shall say unto this mountain, Remove hence to yonder place; and it shall remove; and nothing shall be impossible unto you.* – Matthew 17:20
>
> *And Jesus said..., Go thy way; and as thou hast believed, so be it done unto thee.* – Matthew 8:13
>
> *Now unto him that is able to do exceeding abundantly above all that we ask or think, according to the power that worketh in us...* – Ephesians 3:20

There are no limits placed on what you are able to ask. You are only limited by your desire, faith, belief and persistence.

Expectation

Dream your dream. Expect your dream. Live your dream.

> *...reaching forth unto those things which are before, I press toward the mark...* – Philippians 3:13-14

Every one of us has a goal. Many people have more than one. Sometimes the goal is buried under piles of everyday clutter, often so deep it would take a backhoe to dig it out. These people say, "I'll get to it after I take care of... whatever the distraction may be, or "After I pay off..." whatever the latest debt is. For others, the goal may have been a daydream of "what I want to be when I grow up" that was put aside in childhood because of fear of criticism, doubt about one's ability, or just pushed aside along with other "childhood fantasies."

The point is, everyone has at least one goal. I'm sure you have one too. Something that is important enough to get excited about, to get the juices flowing. Something that makes you wake up enthusiastic about your day, fills you with optimism, inspires you to solve problems, talk to other people, and feel like you are working to accomplish something.

A goal is a powerful thing. Part of its power comes from the feeling it gives you when you think of yourself having achieved the goal. It's great to have a feeling of accomplishment, even if it is a small goal like cleaning out that storage closet in the back room, taking the long summer vacation you have always wanted, or getting the credit card bill paid off. Or it may be larger, like earning a college degree, getting that dream job you've wanted for years, or putting a down payment on your new home. Or it may be changing the world by creating new technology. Whatever the goal is, it gets you excited.

Jesus often taught about goals. He often referred to them as "desires." These are simply things that we want. A desire could also be called "a strong feeling of wanting to have something or wishing for something to happen." When we want some physical object or we want something to happen in our lives, that thing we want is a goal. A goal can be as physical as wanting a house or a pony. Maybe it is a change in your life, like a meaningful relationship, a successful business, or to get into good shape. It could also be something non-physical, like desiring to be optimistic, giving or understanding. Goals can take many shapes, sizes and colors.

> *Therefore I say unto you, What things soever ye desire, when ye pray [ask], believe that ye receive them, and ye shall have them. – Mark 11:24*

> *And all things, whatsoever ye shall ask in prayer, believing, ye shall receive. – Matthew 21:22*

> *Verily, verily, I say unto you, He that believeth on me, the works that I do shall he do also; and greater works than these shall he do; because I go unto my Father. And whatsoever ye shall ask in my name, that will I do… If ye shall ask any thing in my name, I will do it. – John 14:12-14*

Whatever we believe with thought, conviction, emotion and motivation, must come into being. This point is made over and over again by Jesus as he taught.

> *Ye ask, and receive not, because ye ask amiss, that ye may consume it upon your lusts. – James 4:3*

> *…ye shall ask what ye will, and it shall be done unto you. – John 15:7*

Verily, verily, I say unto you, Whatsoever ye shall ask the Father in my name, he will give it you. Hitherto have ye asked nothing in my name: ask, and ye shall receive, that your joy may be full. – John 16:23-24

…ye have not, because ye ask not. – James 4:2

Remember this, even if it is the only thing you remember from this book:

There is absolutely no reason not to ask, and every reason to ask.

A Vision of Success

Walk, and you can see. Climb, and you can see farther. Fly, and you can see beyond the farthest horizon.

What is your greatest desire?

> *He (Abraham) staggered not at the promise of God through unbelief; but was strong in faith, giving glory to God; And being fully persuaded that, what he had promised, he was able also to perform.* – Romans 4:20-22

Abraham knew that God was able to do anything. He did not question it, even in the most challenging situations. Later in life, Abraham was given a vision of all that was his because of his faith.

As a young boy, I was given an allowance from my parents. Twenty-five cents per week. I was expected to budget my money because that was all there was. If I wanted more, I needed to save some of my twenty-five cents each week until it added up. I learned that there was a cap on the amount I would receive, even if I really wanted more. Fortunately, my brother and I had some entrepreneurial ability, and we were able to set up a Kool Aid stand in the summer at the side of the street. This usually brought in another five or ten cents, after expenses, but that was a good portion of my weekly income.

I learned to be frugal, but I also was given the paradigm that there was a ceiling on how much I could earn by working. I learned that I only "deserved" a certain amount. I know better now. I know that Infinite Intelligence has no ceiling. I can ask for anything. Literally, anything. I know that there is an infinite resource, infinite energy, and the ability to respond to anything for which I ask, believing that I have already received it.

When you understand that Infinite Intelligence is able to move the fabric of space and time to make room for your desires and dreams to manifest in reality, you have surpassed the understanding of more than ninety-nine percent of all other people. When you believe that your dreams are already moving into reality, your world will begin to change in ways that you cannot imagine. You will see new opportunities and possibilities where none existed because your perspective has changed. The world will show itself to you in a new way. What used to be problems will become opportunities for learning and expanding your awareness. You will see the other side of the problem, the solution, and pieces of the puzzle that were missing will become evident. Things that were a mystery will be clear and so simple that you will wonder how you ever missed them, and how easily energy flows.

This is a wonderful time. A time full of wonder. You have opened a door to vision, to understanding, and to experiencing the true power of God, Infinite Intelligence, flowing into you, through you, and out to everything around you. You are a creator. You have within you the Kingdom of Heaven, the nature of God. Infinite Intelligence dwells within you. You can ask for anything you desire and it will be given to you in accordance to Laws which Jesus knew about, talked about, and demonstrated thousands of years ago. Those Laws, hidden from most people for centuries, are yours to learn and apply. Abundance, understanding, and the fulfillment of goals are only a matter of asking, seeking and finding.

Forgiveness

Forgiveness is release and freedom.

We know that the subconscious mind is fertile soil in which anything which is planted will grow. One way to gain power and freedom in life is to nurture the growth of forgiveness. This is not the "forgiveness" that is attached to all of the feelings associated with guilt, repentance, confession, and similar things which we have been taught. These feelings only drive us into a small, dark prison of our own making. True forgiveness has to do with letting go of the past. It is the releasing of negative feelings, letting go of feelings that you have been mistreated by someone or some circumstance. In turn, it's releasing the negative feelings that are stewing within you because of holding onto feelings that need to be released.

It is time to let go of anything which does not move you forward toward your goals and dreams. It may mean forgiving yourself, putting your sense of past mistakes and failures aside, and walking away from them. Walking away also means walking toward. It's all a matter of perspective. Walk toward your goal.

Forgiveness is a fragile thing at first, easily squashed or disrupted. But it has very strong healing properties. It is a true anti-toxin. When it is mature, forgiveness is powerful. It can instantly neutralize all of the toxins of the mind.

The power gained by tapping into forgiveness is true power; it is power over all of the crippling paradigms of the past. The freedom gained is also true freedom from the heavy chains and dark prison walls created by anger, resentment and victimization. These emotions are only illusions because they exist only in your mind and have their roots in the past. They are clouds that prevent you from clearly seeing your path or the beautiful vista from beyond the horizon. These negative emotions are like great doors, closed, barred and locked. They hold your mind prisoner, shut out the light of day, and extinguish any hope of communication.

But the locked door, the bars and the key are all on the inside of the prison cell. Forgiveness is the key. You are the only one who can unlock the locks, release the chains, open the doors, and watch as light floods back into your mind as a fresh wind blows away the clouds. Only then can you step out through the doors, renewed and strong, with a free and open mind, to take in the breath of inspiration.

...forgive, and ye shall be forgiven... – Luke 6:37

... lean not unto thine own understanding. – Proverbs 3:5

When you forgive, make it all encompassing. Release people, circumstances and most of all those thoughts within yourself. We all have them. With your power of thought, walk down the old, dark corridors deep within your heart, your subconscious mind, and release those parts of you that have held you back, kept you prisoner. You have the strength. You have the courage. And you have the key in your hand.

Let yourself go. Set yourself free!

Walk out, lift up your eyes, and see the bright vista of possibility and the many birds of opportunity. See your goal and fall in love with it. Whatever you ask, believing, you shall receive.

Now is the time. Today is the day of opportunity. Ask, seek and find.

Photo: Peter Hurley

About the Author

Most of his adult life, the sea has moved him. From surfing in the frigid north Pacific, Dan R. Matthews has been in the ocean from Alaska to the Cape of Good Hope, from the Baltic to the South China Sea. Ever filled with wonder, Dan was a writer from the time he was a child. He has always been in love with words, but not only words. He has a passion for the heavens and the earth too. He learned about why the sky is blue and the sunsets are red, what makes a rainbow, and the way stars live out their lives. He researched many things: the effect of cosmic rays on metals, how organic polymers can be used in new ways, the ecology of marine birds, and advanced energy alternatives.

Through all of his enraptured explorations, he took time to teach others. He helped to open minds and encouraged students to seek answers to the questions of life that we all ask. For seventeen years Dan taught in secondary schools and at the college level. He holds a Master of Science degree, as well as degrees in English and physics. He is a member of American Mensa.

Dan and his wife, Sharen, live on a cliff over the ocean, surrounded by the dense rain forest of the Pacific Northwest. They enjoy surfing and other outdoor activities. Their most important passion is to achieve life goals, with the purpose of helping others.

THE LITERARY FAIRIES

We make your literary wish come true!

Dan R. Matthews

has partnered with

The Literary Fairies

Their mission is to grant literary wishes to those who have experienced or are experiencing an adversity in their life or have a disability and wish to share their story with the world to uplift, inspire and entertain through literacy.

Visit TLF website to find out how YOU could have your literary wish granted or if you wish to make a donation.

More details provided at
www.theliteraryfairies.com

www.ingramcontent.com/pod-product-compliance
Lightning Source LLC
LaVergne TN
LVHW051832080426
835512LV00018B/2842